Alcohol

Alcohol

The guide to healthy drinking by Junius Adams & Michael Leitch.

Omnibus Press

London/New York/Cologne/Sydney

Distributed by Book Sales Limited,
78 Newman Street, London W1P 3LA.
Quick Fox, 33 West 60th Street, New York,
N.Y. 10023, USA.
Book Sales Pty. Limited, 37 Clarendon
Street, Artarmon, Sydney, NSW 2064,
Australia.
Music Sales Gmbh, Kolner Strasse 199,
D-5000 Cologne 90, West Germany.

Editor: Pearce Marchbank
Book design: Pearce Marchbank

First published in different form as 'Drink to Your Health' by Harper & Row, Publishers, Inc. New York.
This edition published 1978 by Omnibus Press, London.

ISBN 0 86001 307 3
Order No. OP 4013 8

Printed in England by Anchor Press Limited,
Tiptree, Essex.

Contents.

Foreword.

This book is a consumer's guide to the act and consequences of drinking, the pleasures and the pitfalls. As such it differs from most other books on drink, which tend to fall into one of three categories. One category considers the joys of a particular branch of alcoholic beverage, usually wine, whisky or beer. Another is concerned with alcoholism and its clinical treatment. The third is a dreadful genre of "comic" book, whose contents seem to have been written in code, and are heavy with knowing passages on the lines of "Wally, as he groped for the communication cord, was manifesting the classic signs of Knebworth's syndrome (q.v.) . . ."

Our book is like none of these. Its aim is to take a careful look at social drinking today. It is written for drinkers with wit enough to know that alcohol is a potentially dangerous substance, but whose everyday lives leave them insufficient time to work out all the ramifications for themselves. The book was first published in the USA, and in preparing a European edition from Junius Adams's original version I have tried to sort out certain difficulties of approach as well as converting American terminology and tables into English usage. For although both countries subscribe to what may be called the Anglo-Saxon approach to alcohol, there are some basic differences, for instance in attitudes to drink and driving, and it has been necessary to make allowance for these.

A word, also, about the tables. There are a number of tables that chart the strength of various drinks and their effect on the consumer. Here, it is important to stress that on neither side of the Atlantic can there be any universally reliable measuring sticks for gauging the effect of alcohol on different individuals. Thus the tables in this book should be seen as approximate illustrations of what may happen, and not as infallible forecasts – rather as one reads a timetable at a station when there is snow on the ground.

Drinking is a serious subject – for many, too serious – but we have tried to maintain a positive approach throughout, taking the view that alcohol is there to be enjoyed rather than avoided. At the same time we have been careful not to minimize the dangers of drinking too heavily. We hope, however, that you will be able to regard the book as a useful companion rather than as a bodyguard.

Michael Leitch

Part one. You, your body, and your drink.

1. When you drink.

With alcohol you come alive; there is euphoria, you are amusing, brilliant; you drop things, you pass out. The slippery slopes of social drinking and how to avoid them.

Alcohol is a versatile and unusual substance. It is a food, containing as many calories, seven per gram, as fat. It is an intoxicating, consciousness-altering drug. And, in large enough quantities, it is a poison which can produce death.

To get an idea of what alcohol does to the body, let's imagine that you're about to swallow a slug of straight whisky or brandy. Before the liquor touches your lips, you've probably inhaled some of its fumes. That inhalation reaches the lungs and is absorbed into the blood. You now have a tiny trace of alcohol in your bloodstream.* Once swallowed, the liquor begins to be absorbed into the blood through the walls of the stomach. Unlike most other foods, alcohol does not need to be digested for the body to use it. It goes to work directly, in its original form. About 20% will be absorbed through the stomach, the rest through the small intestine. Alcohol diffuses very rapidly throughout all the body fluids; just a few minutes after you drink, it will be present in every part of your organism, including the bones.

If you took your drink on an empty stomach, its progress through the body would be swift – which is why one drink before dinner often seems to pack more wallop than two or three afterwards. Food in the stomach, especially fatty or oily foods, will slow down the absorption process. Beer contains food substances which inhibit absorption: the same quantity of alcohol taken in

*It's not just tiny amounts that can be absorbed this way: a persevering person can get quite smashed by inhaling brandy fumes from a snifter glass. One can also absorb alcohol (via enema) through the rectum. Taken rectally, alcohol hits very fast and relatively small amounts will produce drunkenness. The conventional route through the stomach is actually a rather inefficient means of ingestion.

the form of beer or ale will be less intoxicating than when taken as distilled spirits. In other beverages (such as whisky-and-soda, champagne or sparkling wines) the presence of carbon-dioxide bubbles serves to speed the progress of alcohol, because the action of the bubbles tickles the pyloric valve, an organ which monitors the passage of material from the stomach to the intestine, causing it to open wide. This is why one has the feeling of getting drunker more quickly from champagne and other sparkling beverages. On the other hand, if you drink too-large amounts of liquor too quickly, the pylorus will go into spasm, shutting tightly. Nausea and vomiting ensue. This phenomenon probably accounts, at least in part, for the nausea and dizziness usually experienced by neophyte drinkers. The pyloric spasm and ensuing vomiting protects them against larger amounts of alcohol than their tissues can cope with.

As your drink is absorbed in the stomach and small intestine, the veins carry it to the liver, then through the right ventricle of the heart, then to the lungs (where some of it seeps out, giving you "alcohol breath") then to the aorta and from there throughout the body in the arterial circulation. When it reaches the brain, alcohol produces its most significant effect, the one most of us drink it for: an anaesthetic action which dulls the higher centres. Although this is a sedative effect, it feels at first like stimulation. The first drink or two relax the higher brain, bringing a mildly euphoric relaxation of psychic and physical tension. Along with this comes a feeling of warmth, caused by a slight elevation of pulse rate and blood pressure. Blood rushes into the capillaries, dilating them, and this in turn warms the skin.

This warming effect is merely temporary: liquor in fact causes a heat loss, because it brings warmth to the surface of the body and thus dissipates it more rapidly than usual. Blood pressure, initially raised by the increased action of the heart, then becomes reduced as the blood vessels expand.

About 10% of the alcohol in the body is eliminated through the urine and the breath. The rest has to be oxidized (digested). Whereas food substances such as sugar or fat can be oxidized by tissues throughout the body, alcohol is digested only in the liver, a drop or two at a time. The average liver oxidizes approximately ½ oz per hour – the equivalent of just over 1 oz of 70% proof spirits (one single whisky or ½ pint of beer). The alcohol is first converted to acetaldehyde, a rather toxic substance, which is in turn quickly converted to "acetate", a basic energy source which can be used by all the body tissues. When the "acetate" is then oxidized, the final products are water and carbon dioxide.

Since the maximum amount of alcohol that can be eliminated by the body is about ½ oz per hour, any amount more than this is retained in the body, causing drunkenness, which increases with the amounts ingested. The mechanism by which alcohol affects the brain to produce intoxication has never been fully understood, but the stages of drunkenness are known. The first few doses of alcohol produce a mild anaesthesia in the higher or "new" brain – that section which controls the function Freudians refer to as the superego. This part of the brain appears to contain and generate messages pertaining to caution, self-criticism, self-doubt, anxiety, over-sensitivity to social pressures, over-reaction to pain, and so on. This initial anaesthesia makes the drinker feel warm, mentally relaxed, often better able to display his skills and wit, less concerned with pain, irritations, inhibitions or restraints. More alcohol will further dampen the higher centres, producing an obvious relaxation of inhibitions, euphoria (though sometimes nastiness or moroseness), exaggerated emotion, displays of amorousness, aggression or outrageous humour.

At this point the higher brain centres are decidedly depressed. More liquor will now begin to affect those centres which control motor functions. The next stage produces clumsiness and impaired coordination, unsteadiness in walking or standing, and a tendency to primitive, gross, uncouth or uncontrollable behaviour (the higher brain is now virtually asleep). Still more liquor will produce obvious incoordination of the motor functions, with considerable stumbling and falling down, and mental impairment to the point of incoherence. With another drink or two, the person will almost invariably pass out in a semi-stupor. If he ingests still more alcohol, he will fall into a state of general anaesthesia or coma. A really large additional dose will produce death by anaesthetizing that part of the brain that controls respiration. This lethal effect of alcohol, by stopping respiration, is identical to the lethal effects of other anaesthetic agents, such as opiates, barbiturates or ether.

Cases of death by drinking are fortunately rare. Habitual drunks, accustomed as they are to ingesting huge amounts of alcohol, sometimes manage to take one last lethal dose just before passing out. Other deaths occur as the result of a bet: a show-off drinker will wager that he can drink x amount of drinks within y

number of minutes and will drop dead after his performance. His mistake was not in the amount of liquor consumed – ordinarily he could probably handle it – but in the precipitateness with which he drank it. When you gulp liquor instead of sipping it, the effects are much more severe.

The strength of alcohol.

Alcoholic drinks are made by adding yeast to ferment the sugary materials that exist naturally in plants. The alcohol so produced is ethyl alcohol, and this is the only safe form of alcohol for human consumption. Beers are made from barley, wine from grapes, cider from apples, etc. These are relatively weak in alcohol, but the strength of drinks made from the same raw materials can be greatly increased by a secondary process, distilling, in which the liquor is boiled again and the vapour collected and allowed to cool and reliquefy.

We, however, need not concern ourselves unduly with the skills of distiller, vigneron and brewer, admirable though they are. This book is primarily devoted to the pleasures and other effects of social drinking, and the important thing to remember is that alcohol is a fast-acting intoxicant. It is therefore advisable to know in advance how strong a particular drink is likely to be.

Measuring Systems.

There are three main systems of measuring strength: the British (Sikes), European (Gay-Lussac), and American. These record strengths on a relative scale of 40° European: 80° American: 70° British. Of these systems, the Gay-Lussac is the easiest to understand, since it simply describes the percentage of pure or absolute alcohol – 40%, for example, being fairly standard for spirits, e.g. whisky, gin, brandy and rum (vodka is usually somewhat weaker). The American system differs only in that the degree figure is doubled; a bottle of 80° US proof will therefore contain 40% alcohol. The British system, on the other hand, assesses strength according to "proof spirit".

The term "proof spirit" relates to the centuries-old method that distillers used to gauge the concentration of alcohol in water. Gunpowder was added to the mixture: if it ignited, this meant that the mixture was roughly half and half, or more; if there was too much water the mixture would not ignite. A spirit was thereby tested and "proven". Proof spirit today is a mixture of 57.1% spirit by volume and 42.9% water. A spirit may also be described as 100% proof, meaning that it contains 100% of the spirit/water mixture. If you buy a bottle of, say, gin marked 70° proof, this should contain 70% of spirit of proof strength, i.e. 40% absolute alcohol and 60% water by volume.

Depending in which part of the world you find yourself, the ratio of 40:80:70 can be applied to calculate the comparative strengths of all kinds of alcoholic drinks. Below is a table showing the average strengths of various popular drinks in relation to one another, and the amount of each that contains approximately ½ oz of absolute alcohol (the amount that the liver can oxidize in one hour – see page 12).

How strong is your drink?

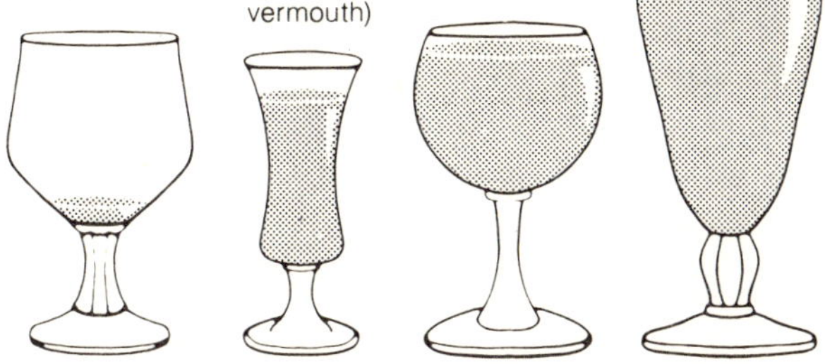

	Spirits (whisky, gin, rum, brandy, vodka)	Fortified and flavoured wines (sherry, port, madeira, vermouth)	Table wine	Beer, cider (medium strength)
Strength British ° proof	65°-70°	30°-35°	20°	8°
Percentage of absolute alcohol	37%-40%	17%-20%	11%	4½%
Equivalent to ½ oz absolute alcohol	1 single pub measure	1 pub measure	1/7 bottle	½ pint

How drunk is drunk?

Body weight and blood alcohol levels.

The amount of alcohol present in the blood is often used as an indicator of how much liquor a person has ingested and thus, presumably, of how drunk he is. The official abbreviation for this is BAC, or blood alcohol concentration. Sometimes, as in tests for drunken driving, the breath or urine is tested instead; the resulting figure will be identical with the BAC, since alcohol is diffused equally throughout the body fluids. Since 1967 it has been an offence in Britain to drive a car with a BAC of more than 80 milligrams per 100 millilitres. By the time the police were on the point of introducing their breathalyzer tests, this statistic had sunk deep into the national consciousness, so deep in fact that its actual meaning has tended to remain obscure, blotted out perhaps by the overriding stresses of the moment, the sudden conviction that "All that matters is whether I lose my licence".

It is doubly interesting, therefore, to see this awesome marker-point of 80 mg in the context of other BACs, and to look at some of the physical effects that can be expected at each of the various stages discussed above.

Blood Alcohol Concentration.

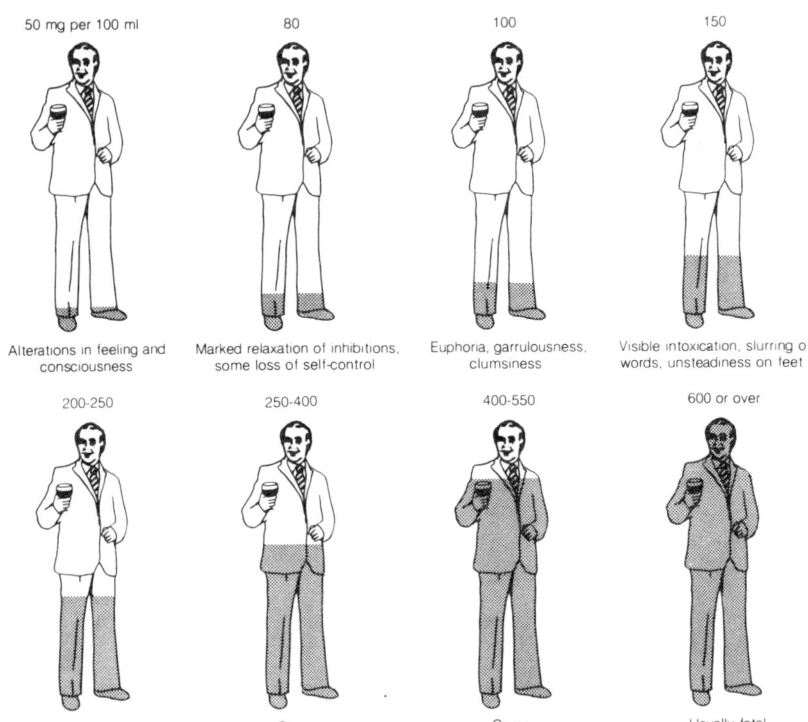

The question that naturally arises next is: how many drinks produce these levels? Here there are so many variables that it is very difficult to set out a table that will be valid for all. The principal differences in people's drinking capacities have to do with their tolerance to alcohol, their mood and state of health, their food intake, and their body weight. To take only the latter type of difference, it is clear that since the BAC is an index of how much alcohol is present in the body fluids, the amount of alcohol will relate to the volume of the person's body fluids, and hence to their size. And, since a woman's body is made up of only 55%-65% water, as opposed to 65%-75% for a man, women need less drink than men to reach the same BAC. The following tables show the approximate number of drinks required to reach a given state.

How many drinks?

Weight (stones)	Number of drinks
BAC of 50 mg per 100 ml	
7-10	1-2 single whiskies, or 1-2 pints of beer or cider, etc.
10-12	2-3 whiskies or 1-1½ pints
12-14	3-6 whiskies or 1½-3 pints
over 14	4-8 whiskies or 2-4 pints
BAC of 80 mg per 100 ml	
7-10	3-6 whiskies or 1½-3 pints
10-12	3-8 whiskies or 1½-4 pints
12-14	4-8 whiskies or 2-4 pints
over 14	6+ whiskies or 3+ pints
BAC of 150 mg per 100 ml	
7-10	6+ whiskies or 3+ pints
10-12	8+ whiskies or 4+ pints
12-14	10+ whiskies or 5+ pints
over 14	12+ whiskies or 6+ pints

These figures apply to amounts of drink ingested in a relatively short time – say 1-3 hours (beer drinkers will tend to take longer than whisky drinkers). They reveal a dramatic difference according to size. The amount needed to make the 7-10 stone person drunk may have little effect on the 14 stone drinker. Reverse this and give the lightweight drinker the 12+ whiskies needed to make the big person drunk, and he or she might end up virtually comatose, with a BAC in the region of 400.

At the same time, readers should take these figures as general indications rather than as firm directives. Some large people can drink very little, while some near-midgets have apparently bottomless stomachs and strong heads to match. It would, too, be irresponsible to suggest that there are low limits beneath which one will always be sober. It is a simple fact that drinking *always* alters the conscious state of the drinker. Thus the efficiency of a car driver – to mention one particularly contentious area – will always be impaired by alcohol.

Tolerance to alcohol.

The body-weight tables above are cautiously broad in the numbers of drinks they prescribe. This is because drinkers vary enormously in their capacities, and here one of the most important factors is the tolerance that a drinker can develop for alcohol in general and his or her favourite kind(s) of drink in particular.

If you serve several alcoholic drinks to someone who has never drunk before he or she will probably show all the signs of advanced intoxication: dizziness and incoordination, maudlin or extravagant behaviour, perhaps also nausea and vomiting. This may seem like a purely physiological reaction, but it is not; the same thing happens to people getting high on marijuana for the first time. Both groups cannot handle the flood of new sensations assaulting their consciousness, and respond in an exaggerated way (like a "drunken sailor"). It is the consciousness-altering characteristics that produce such uncontrolled reactions.

After the neophyte drinker has had more experience, he no longer reacts so quickly, and can remain relatively sober on two or three times the alcohol that rendered him helpless during his first few drinking experiences. If he now goes on to become a seasoned drinker who can "hold his liquor", he will be able to act and talk with seeming sobriety while maintaining a BAC that would put less-experienced drinkers under the table. The drunken state is a new mode of existence that can be learned. Just as a newborn baby, unable at first to coordinate any of his movements, learns eventually to grasp with his hands, then stand up, then walk and talk, then operate computers or space vehicles, so the drunk, given sufficient experience, can learn to cope with his state. In his vaudeville days, for instance, W. C. Fields was able to perform six acts daily of intricate jugglery while on a one-to-two-quarts-of-gin-per-day drinking regime. Fields had "learned" the drunken state and could function within it.

This type of acquired tolerance is referred to as psychological or behavioural tolerance. It is the main form of habituation that drinkers acquire. Chronic extra-heavy drinkers can also acquire tissue tolerance. In experiments with heavy drinkers, Drs Jack H. Mendelson and Joseph La Dou of Harvard Medical School discovered that "when subjects were receiving 30 oz (of liquor) per 24 hours the degree of intoxication was surprisingly small. Similarly, the serum alcohol levels were lower than would be expected." In other words, the bodies of chronic heavy drinkers have found ways to metabolize alcohol more efficiently than is usual. That tissue tolerance does exist is corroborated by the fact that ultra-heavy drinkers also show a "cross-resistance" to anaesthetics such as ether and chloroform. As the well-known authority on alcoholism, Dr E. M. Jellinek, says, "It is the common experience of surgeons that alcoholic patients require much more of these substances than do others in order to produce surgical anaesthesia." Tissue tolerance does not extend very far. Dr Mendelson found that the same subjects who thrived on 30 oz per day had trouble when their dosage was increased to 40 oz. Dr Mendelson suggests that for men there may be a sort of natural limit of one quart (32 oz) per day which it is dangerous to go beyond; it seems that the act of opening a new bottle is likely to pose the irresistible temptation to "kill" that one too (in Britain the same principle probably applies to our standard spirit bottle, even though, at 26.67 oz, it is a good deal smaller than the American quart).

The up-curve and the down-curve.

Liquor feels a lot better while it's taking effect than while it's wearing off – especially if you're drinking a lot. A person getting high feels exhilarated, confident, relaxed, energetic – he's getting the stimulant effect of alcohol. Coming down from his high, he's apt to feel dull, drowsy and out of sorts – the depressant effects are now revealed. At the same time he may still be able to perform fairly intricate tasks. This is one of the deceptive aspects of the drinking experience. On his up-curve, the drinker feels he is gloriously alive and capable; on the way down, he feels inept and zombie-esque. Yet actually the reverse is true, as can be demonstrated by experiment. Drs Ben Morgan Jones and Oscar A. Parsons, of the University of Oklahoma Health Sciences Center, for instance, tested a group of drinkers with a series of verbal puzzles and found that their performance was more impaired "while transcending into the alcohol state than while sinking back to earth". In another study they found that drinkers had poorer short-term memories while getting drunk than while sobering up, even when their blood alcohol levels were the same.

Drinking in time with our biological clock.
Few drinkers who are not actually alcoholics want to drink first thing in the morning – just before breakfast, say – the very thought is nauseating. Before lunch, though, a drink is much more possible – even if the first sip of strong liquor provokes an uncomfortable shudder. However, the first drink of the evening is a far more inviting prospect. By then we are fully set up and ready for it. Is this just a matter of habit, of social conditioning? Probably not.

In her book *Body Time*, Gay Gaer Luce tells about an experiment in which mice were injected with a quantity of alcohol equivalent to one quart of vodka for a human being. When the mice were given the alcohol early in the day, around their usual time of awakening, 60% of them died. The same dose given as a nightcap, close to their time of rest, killed only 12%. Not totally conclusive, by any means, but I believe that more or less the same pattern holds true for human beings. The person who waits until sundown to start drinking is more in tune with the tides of life than the one who starts first thing in the morning.

Stages of drunkenness.
Since we're going to be discussing the various stages of drunkenness throughout this book, it's probably a good idea to emphasize them right now so that we know what we're talking about. For our purposes, it will be sufficient to distinguish four different stages . . .
Stage One (BAC 50) Mild euphoria, slight relaxation of tensions and inhibitions, feelings of warmth and cheerfulness. No overt signs of drunkenness.
Stage Two (BAC 80) Marked relaxation of inhibitions, expansive, talkative, sociable, may be noticeably "under the influence".
Stage Three (BAC 100+) Definite drunkenness, with at least some clumsiness due to impaired motor functions. More or less unrestrained acting-out of sociable, aggressive or amorous impulses. Heightened emotionalism.
Stage Four (BAC 150+) Befuddled condition, markedly clumsy, incoherent, semi-comatose.

It has often been stated that people drink because they like the personality changes that alcohol brings them. This notion is certainly borne out by my interviews with drinkers. Almost unanimously, they felt that being in Stage One or Stage Two gave them a personality or social presence which was more effective and pleasurable than their normal cold-sober one.

These stages of drunkenness can also be used to define different types of drinkers. The Stage One drinker is a moderate social drinker who enjoys the mildly relaxing effects of taking a drink or two but does not seek or relish drunkenness in any form. If the Stage One drinker takes a few too many and slides into Stage Two, he may have a feeling of having transgressed and of having made a fool of himself. He has no particular desire to lapse from sobriety.

The Stage Two drinker enjoys the expansiveness and seeming emotional freedom he finds in the semi-drunken state. He feels confident, witty, jovial, better able to express himself and to function in a group. Many Stage Two drinkers are people who find alcohol a help to them in their occupation: the salesman who discovers he can approach people more easily and deliver a better sales pitch with a few drinks under his belt, the jazz musician who finds he can play with more verve and attempt more daring improvisations, the night-club comic who finds it easier to make people laugh when he has consumed some bottled hilarity. Being in Stage Two can be helpful to people whose effectiveness is enhanced by heightened emotionalism and sociability or fancifulness and exaggeration in verbal communications. The writer, the actor, the political orator can often find inspiration in the bottle. Nuclear physicists, chartered accountants or diamond cutters, on the other hand, are probably better advised to do their drinking outside of working hours.

The Stage Three drinker is someone who perhaps feels cut off from his deeper self, and finds that alcohol enables him to tap emotions and impulses that are not otherwise available to him. As one heavy drinker said to me, "It may be an illusion, but getting smashed makes me feel whole again. I can say what I really mean, feel what I really feel." Primitive societies, for whom drinking is a religious ritual, prize the condition of Stage Three or thereabouts as being a holy or ecstatic state. (Perhaps the generally less primitive British pubgoer, convening with friends and acquaintances in the ordered, conservative atmosphere of his local and there downing glasses of light and bitter, or whatever, until everyone gets darkly exalted or passionate and declamatory, is himself performing an unconscious quasi-religious rite.)*

Stage Three encourages far-out or exhibitionist behaviour. The drunk who steps out into a busy street and starts directing traffic, the woman who goes wild and throws off her clothes** are Stage Three personalities. A number of drinkers reported to me that they like Stage Three because it inspires them sexually, making them more direct, passionate or flamboyant in bed.

The Stage Four drinker, or drunk, drinks in order to blot out consciousness entirely. This activity may represent a desire to return to the womb, as some psychoanalysts have suggested. Or it may simply be a quite understandable attempt to escape from present circumstances, as with the derelict sleeping rough, often in the malodorous company of other derelicts. Some Stage Four drinkers, of course, are respectable, well-heeled citizens who drink themselves into near-extinction in the privacy of their own homes. Every heavy drinker experiences Stage Four at times, but the true Stage Four drinker is someone who habitually uses alcohol to achieve oblivion and gets there rapidly, without enjoying the first three stages.

For any given individual the stages of drunkenness resemble different personalities, each exhibiting traits not necessarily found in the individual's sober personality. Someone who is normally polite, tactful and reserved, for instance, may become blunt, aggressive and outspoken in Stage Two or Stage Three. A normally kind and thoughtful person can become cold and unfeeling, just as a cold, repressive type may wax warm and solicitous. The more time a drinker spends in his alternate personality, the more that personality develops a life, character and history all its own. Research into what is called "state-dependent" learning suggests that this alternate personality phenomenon may be something that is common to all animal life. One researcher, Donald Overton, demonstrated that when rats are trained under the influence of a drug, they remember what they learned better when put back into the same drugged state than when undrugged or drugged with some other substance. The same experiment was done with humans, using alcohol as the drug, and the human subjects performed in the same way the rats did – when trained in a task after drinking alcohol, they remembered their training better after

*This would not necessarily put him in Stage Three.

**I have not witnessed this except in foreign films (UK editor).

having drunk again than when they were sober.

The drunken millionaire in Charlie Chaplin's *City Lights* is a perfect example of the alternate personality. When drunk, he feels Charlie is his great buddy; he lavishes presents on him, takes him out to night clubs, throws parties for him. But when he wakes up sober he has no memory of Chaplin and has him thrown out of the house. As soon as he is drunk again, Chaplin is his dear friend once more.

The blackout.
A drinker will have no difficulty remembering what happened while he was in Stage One, and seldom will forget his Stage Two experiences, but there will be memory lapses – ranging from slight to almost total – in Stage Three or Four drunkenness. In his movie *The Bank Dick*, W. C. Fields asks a bartender, "Was I in here last night, and did I spend a twenty-dollar bill?" On being told yes, Fields says, "Thank goodness, I thought I'd lost it!" Frequently, drinkers cannot remember who drove them home the night before, how they got to bed, whether or not they had sex with their spouses, and so on. In another anecdote, a man wakes up in a hotel room with an appalling hangover to find, sleeping peacefully beside him, an extremely ugly woman. He groans, gets out of bed quietly, dresses, puts twenty pounds on the bedside table and is starting to walk out when he feels a tug at his trouser leg. He looks down and sees a woman who is even uglier than the one in bed. She gazes up at him and says, "How about something for the bridesmaid?"

Evidence that such blackouts are not just the fabrications of scriptwriters or that odder social group, the people who invent jokes, is provided by a *New York Magazine* article on alcoholic New York City policemen. The article describes how a young patrolman came to in a hotel room in the Caribbean with a strange woman he had just married; his last memory was of going out to a bar in Queens for a couple of beers – over a week previously.

The more tolerance the drinker acquires for alcohol, the more likely he is to have blackouts: in time he may be able to remain on his feet and function with some efficiency after taking on a dose of alcohol that would put a less tolerant drinker to sleep. The blackout may obliterate scattered memories only, or it may cover hours and even days. It is similar to sleepwalking or a trance. The conscious personality is asleep, and a secondary personality takes over. Sometimes the blacked-out person will appear quite lucid and normal to people around him, able to take part in group activities and engage in seemingly intelligent conversations, but the next day he will remember nothing. Having an extended blackout is often a spooky and unsettling experience. Many drinkers become quite frightened after "losing" a few hours the night before and take the pledge, seek psychiatric help, or join Alcoholics Anonymous. It is not a comfortable thought to realize that the self is so feeble that it can be obliterated by a pint or two of liquor, leaving the body under the control of what seems like an alien personality.

Why we drink too much.
Light and moderate drinkers seldom go out of control, except perhaps on occasions when they are coerced into drunkenness by heavier-drinking companions. But the drinker who sets out to achieve Stage Two or Stage Three may find that he continues drinking after he has reached his goal. The trouble is that, once he has reached a certain state of drunkenness, he is no longer the same person who had earlier decided, "I'll have three [or six] drinks – no more". As an old Japanese proverb says, "First the man takes a drink, then the drink takes a drink, then the drink takes the man."

Sober, the drinker has all his inhibitory mechanisms in working order. He can decide to take just one drink and stick to his decision. Deciding to take five drinks but not six poses problems, however. After the five drinks, he is not the sober fellow who resolved to be moderate. He's feeling elated, expansive, daring if not reckless. He may have a clear memory of his earlier resolve, but it no longer seems very relevant to his present condition. So he goes ahead and has more drinks. Moderating one's drinking cannot usually be achieved by making sterner resolves while sober. It has to be accomplished by training the drunken personality to be more moderate. Ways in which this training may be done will be discussed in Part III.

Effects of excessive drinking.

Much of this will be covered in subsequent chapters, but let's summarize here what tends to happen when we drink too much. The heavy drinker has trained his body to accept large amounts of alcohol. Since alcohol is a food, his body learns to metabolize it along with the other food it is given. This it does quite efficiently, but at some cost to itself, since alcohol contains none of the vitamins, minerals and other essential nutriments found in normal food. A deficit of these substances begins to occur. This deficit and its accompanying discomforts are interpreted by the drinker not as a need for better food and more vitamins, but as a need for more alcohol. This he proceeds to take, thereby aggravating his condition still further. Along the way, his social and domestic life turns into a disaster area. Family relationships are ruined, he becomes unemployable, and estranges himself from all but his closest friends – some of whom will also feel unable to tolerate his company on other than special or rare occasions.

If he continues on this downward course, he may end up as a terminal alcoholic who has virtually abandoned food and subsists on booze alone. Along the way, he will have acquired an actual physical addiction to alcohol: he cannot stop drinking without suffering withdrawal symptoms, which may include delirium tremens (a hallucinatory state in which the patient shakes, trembles, or moves agitatedly about while seeing or hearing bizarre sights and sounds). He will probably suffer from alcoholic polyneuritis, a vitamin-deficiency disease characterized by multiple aches and pains, irritability, sensory disturbances and impaired reflexes. If he persists in his drinking, he may fall into Wernicke's encephalopathy, a helpless stupor compounded by paralysis of the eyes, or Korsakoff's syndrome, a condition in which the memory fails and the patient becomes confused and disorientated. These are just some of the severe disorders that can mark the progress into decay of the vitamin-starved alcoholic.

2. The benefits of drinking.

Why you (and other people) drink; the good it can do you. National attitudes and prejudices. What the pro-alcohol doctors believe.

This book is based in part on my own experiences with alcohol and on the experiences of about fifty other drinkers with whom I had lengthy formal interviews. In the main my informants were healthy, prosperous middle-class people, all of them moderate-to-heavy drinkers – businessmen and business-women, housewives, people in the professions, the arts, the media, politics, finance. Most of them were in what I would call young middle age, and had been drinking for about fifteen to twenty years. I discussed with them their drinking habits, health problems if any, social lives, sex lives, hangovers, unusual experiences with alcohol, etc. One of the questions I asked was, "What do you like about alcohol, what do you find good or helpful about it, why do you drink?"

Many of the answers were on one general theme, the theme of sociability. People drink because drinking is a friendly activity. It relaxes us, draws us closer together, helps us be lively and have fun, serves as a social solvent in gatherings that would otherwise make us feel awkward or standoffish, helps bring the shy or inhibited individual out of his shell. There were a number of variations within this theme.

Drinking as an antidote to shyness.

Many people, particularly young people, find liquor a big help in overcoming shyness or awkwardness or a feeling of being out of place. Here's how one woman put it:

"I used to say liquor was my best friend because I was always shy, I could never talk to anybody. I always felt stupid and unable to speak. Then I discovered drinking when I was sixteen or seventeen, and suddenly I became like those other kids who were always talking to everybody. And then I could converse with people, join

in. I was raised in such a Victorian way. I was so inhibited, still am. That's something I've had to fight all my life. I don't think I would ever have gotten out of Portland if I hadn't started drinking."

A middle-aged male:

"I was very tense and ill-at-ease as a young man. Partly this was because of being brought up in a peculiar situation – eccentric mother, no father in the family – partly because I spent so many years in Europe. When I came back I felt out of place – not really American. It was difficult for me to feel at home or meet people or make friends. Then I began drinking, going to bars, cocktail parties. I made a lot of friends, had a succession of love affairs with girls. Actually I didn't like liquor then. It was just a means to an end – socializing, meeting people. It helped me over a difficult period, it really did. After a few drinks I was no longer afraid of people, of what they might think of me. I still drink – I do like it now – but I don't need it to feel confident."

A woman in her fifties:

"I think drinking sort of quickens the mind, if you don't have too much. Then it does the reverse. I've never understood why they call it a depressant. I consider it the other thing. What's the word? Stimulant. My mind starts going a little more lively. Sometimes I think of things to say that I might be too inhibited to think of otherwise. It takes me out of my shell. I'm not afraid to join the group."

Drinking as a social solvent.

Almost every one of my informants talked about now liquor promoted conviviality and good feeling, helped people "break the ice" and reach out to each other. One man said:

"I associate alcohol with graciousness, the tradition of offering people something. That's why I seldom have a drink when I'm alone. I think that in any profession that requires people getting to know each other drinking is important. A long session of drinking and talking creates a bond. It's like the handshake. Shaking hands originally showed you had no weapons concealed. Drinking shows you've got nothing to hide. It's sort of a sign of trust. Without drinking I wouldn't have got to know so many people so well."

A number of people mentioned how unpleasant it is to go to parties or gatherings where no liquor is served. This is a subject on which drinkers are constantly being maligned. "If you need a drink to be sociable, that's not social drinking," says an anti-liquor pamphlet put out by the Jay Cees. Baloney! The average drinker may not be an open, spontaneously friendly person, but at least he's trying to become one. I've been to all too many gatherings of good God-fearing teetotallers where everybody sat around like sticks, once in a while interrupting the silence with remarks like "Looks like rain", or "I see by the papers that . . . " until everyone felt almost dead from boredom or embarrassment. At times like that I do wish for a drink, desperately, and I wish they would take one too. But when I'm in a room full of people who are alive, friendly, trusting, vibrant, I don't miss liquor or resent their not serving it.

A public-relations man:
"No way. You've got to have liquor when you give a press party. It loosens people up, makes them receptive. I did a couple of promotions once for a fellow who was some kind of temperance nut or something. He wouldn't let us serve booze, coffee or tea, just some stupid fruit punch. Can you imagine trying to keep a hundred press people happy on nothing but fruit punch? Hell, I couldn't keep them in the room! They started leaving before we even began our presentation."

Booze and the business lunch.
Cartoonists make fun of the heavy business lunch, economists complain about the millions invested in it, and employers bemoan the man-hours lost because of the drunkenness of the participants, yet the business lunch goes on and on. I can't speak for any other branches of industry, but as a former magazine editor and veteran of many hundreds of "literary" lunches I can attest that their value to the publishing business is incalculable. If liquor were banned tomorrow, the whole industry would collapse.

When the lunch is with a non-drinker, particularly one who's reserved, formal or stuffy, you discuss whatever you came to discuss, make a little small talk, then pay the bill and get out of the restaurant fast. Not so with the alcoholic lunch. Often the person you're meeting is a stranger or someone you only know as a voice on the telephone. But liquor makes for swift intimacy, and by the time you've had a few drinks you may start exchanging deep personal confidences and making delightfully wicked gossip about other people in the business. When you leave you feel you've made a friend for life – and sometimes you have. More important to your employer, you've made a valuable connection that will enable you to do business on a more personal and friendly basis in the future.

Liquor and the creative person.

Performers and people in the arts often find that liquor helps them be more creative. I was once friendly with a night-club comic who deliberately got two-thirds drunk every night before he went out to do his act. The drunkenness helped him to ad-lib and free-associate witticisms in a way he couldn't have achieved otherwise. When he wasn't working, he had no interest in liquor. I never saw him take a drink on his day off.

A couple of my interviewees mentioned using alcohol for inspiration.

Well-known jazz trumpet-player:

"I tend to drink occasionally when I'm playing the horn, which is when I do my heaviest drinking really. I'll have a couple of beers when I'm playing the horn. And then I'll switch to Scotch and have maybe two or three of those before the end of the evening. That gets me to a good place for playing the horn. It's not a place I would particularly enjoy if I were just at a social thing. I don't drink very much socially any more. You tend to get fatigued toward the end of a long evening playing the horn, and drinking rests you, gives you a sense of well-being. I can see where jazz musicians who very often get bored by what they're doing, especially if they're playing the same club every night, would tend to overdrink. A lot of these guys turn into lushes, I think, just because they're trying to . . . you know, you're kind of faced with an impossible problem as a performing jazz musician where you're supposed to crank out the best you have creatively on call. Endlessly. So you turn to something else to fuel the creative instinct or turn off the pain or something. I don't know. Anyhow, it helps."

A writer:

"Usually I never drink when I'm working, but once in a while I do. It's not that I'm feeling blocked or discouraged or anything. It's – I don't know, perhaps I feel I'm too self-critical. I've done some rather surprising things when practically dead drunk – surprising to me, anyway. Of course they need a lot of editing. And I feel ghastly the next day."

Drinking as a consciousness alterer.
Several of my informants said they liked drinking because it puts them into an alternate state of mind or consciousness.

One of them said:
"It's like going to another country. It's one way of . . . travelling without leaving, physically. It's closely related, too, I think, to music. It gives you some sort of release. Also I like it, the social ambience of it. I like a bar scene which is impersonal and yet there is some sociability there. You meet people and feel good. It's a non-traumatic experience. Whereas, you know, jobs and so many other things are."

Alcohol and sex.
In interviews with 43 drinkers, 24 men and 19 women, I asked how alcohol affected their sex lives. Of the men, 3 reported that drinking takes away performance (for days after a drinking bout, said one man); 4 found drinking a deterrent to sex and said that it made sex unappealing or unaesthetic; 2 reported that drinking slowed their orgasms too much, so that their partners became worn out; and 15 said that drinking made them more active sexually. Of the women, 2 reported that although drinking made them more amorous and adventurous it also inhibited performance; 3 said drinking made "no difference"; and 14 felt that drinking improved and enhanced sex.

Some comments by my women interviewees:
"It makes me more amorous, definitely."
"I get more creative in bed, better able to express myself."
"Sex drunk is different from sex sober. I get more lively and versatile, try things that I wouldn't ordinarily."
"It relaxes me and makes me feel more open to the experience."
"If anything, it makes me more horny."
"I get more adventurous but I don't go through with it. I'd like to go looking for adventure but then I have a personality change that gets in the way before anything happens."

Some by my men interviewees:
"Drinking on sex life is negative. I mean sex has to have a degree of sensitivity to it, so neither one of you can be loaded. There's no fun screwing a drunken broad, even if she's your wife."
"Liquor is a turn-on. Get stoned enough and you're practically a walking Id. And when Id meets Id, watch out. Sober, I'll see a pretty girl across the room and feel a twinge of lust which I do

nothing about. Stoned, I may easily walk right over and start necking with her."
"It releases my inhibitions and turns me into a more sexual person. Without drinks, my tendency would be to come too fast and be a dissatisfying mate in that respect. Liquor slows down the response there. It's definitely congenial to good sexual relationships."
"A little bit of it helps as a relaxant, I think. But there's a communications thing that ought to happen and if either party or both overdrink, the quality of the communication suffers."

To summarize these views, which in essence expand the "social solvent" theme discussed earlier, drink is a successful relaxant for those who enjoy it and can, either taken alone or with a pleasant meal, lubricate sexual desire. On occasion, as Shakespeare's porter observed in *Macbeth,* "It provokes the desire, but takes away the performance." Equally though, heavy drinking accompanied by an increased tolerance for alcohol can lead to heavier, i.e. more, sex.

How drinkers feel about liquor.
Many drinkers act as if they think drinking is a hilarious, often ridiculous pastime. They kid each other about how drunk they get, tell stories about how so-and-so passed out in a bed of nettles or went swimming with all his clothes on, and so forth. In my interviews, however, I asked rather serious questions and got serious answers in return. A surprising number of people revealed rather deep feelings about liquor and drinking. Drinking has a value to them which they never discuss ordinarily, perhaps because it is too important, too basic.

I think that most, perhaps all, drinkers drink as a life-affirming act – a quest for love, a reaching-out towards one's fellow man.

National attitudes.

The views of the people quoted above are typical of the Anglo-Saxon approach to alcohol. It is an approach commonly found in countries where beer and spirits are the most popular alcoholic drinks, and where wine is regarded as a pleasant experience associated in the main with special occasions.* In both Britain and the USA the pattern of drinking is non-continuous: normal social

*This notion is changing, and wine-drinking at the weekends, if not more regularly, has become a prevalent facet of British middle-class life.

drinking occurs at regular, well-spaced intervals, either at the midday break, or at the end of the day's work, or as a prelude and accompaniment to the evening meal, or as a way of relaxing during the evening, often in the shared surroundings of a pub, bar or club.

A third common factor is the rate of drinking. British and American social drinkers take their alcohol relatively fast, the aim being rapidly to induce an altered state of consciousness in which they will feel more relaxed and sociable. This method of drinking, unless controlled, is likely to lead to drunkenness either through excessive speed of intake in the initial phase or simply through drinking more than the body can cope with in the period allowed for drinking. The "panic" that in Britain can take hold in the half-hour before the pubs shut produces many casualties of the latter type.

In wine-growing countries such as Italy and France, millions of people earn their living from the production and sale of alcoholic drinks. As many as a third of French adults are involved in the drinks business, while in Italy some 10% of all arable land is set aside for viticulture, more than in France. In the warm and sunny climate of these and other wine-growing lands, drinking goes on regularly throughout the day. Large quantities are consumed every 24 hours, and there is a strong tradition of drinking at meal-times within the family unit. A steady pattern of absorption is therefore the rule, rather than the more jagged highs and lows that characterize the graph of the Anglo-Saxon drinker.

Because alcohol in these wine-growing countries is so easy to obtain and also cheap, especially in the form of wine, aperitifs and digestives, it has assumed a much greater importance in the national cultures and in family life, and is used, for example, as a tonic and a cure-all for numerous minor illnesses. In this atmosphere people are reluctant to accept that the regular ingestion of large amounts of alcohol can be harmful, and any questioning of the habit is likely to be treated with hostility. An extreme, though useful, illustration of this attitude is the true story of a French girl, aged three, who complained of seeing "toads and big fish" in her bed. At first, doctors thought she was epileptic, then it emerged that she was being given two large glasses of wine a day. Advised to exchange the wine for a glass of water the mother, horrified, said, "Tap water? And what about the microbes?"*

*The mother's horror of water might have been well founded in previous centuries, and probably was, but in modern France such views are eccentric.

Both the Anglo-Saxon and wine-growing (mostly Latin) schools of drinking use alcohol for pleasure as well as release. The taste of a drink, especially of wines and wine-derived drinks, has encouraged the filling of miles of bookshelves with a very special and mostly, no doubt, informed literature. Beer and whisky drinkers, too, can be very finicky and critical of the product set before them, though only in extreme circumstances will they decline to consume it. The point, however, is that taste and the consideration of taste play important roles in the attitudes to alcohol that prevail in these geographical regions. A different outlook altogether holds sway in the countries comprising the "hard-liquor zone", which includes Poland, Russia, Iceland, Norway, Sweden and Finland. Here alcohol is used not as a pleasure-giving stimulant but as an intoxicant, a quick and convenient road to oblivion.

As a means of alleviating social stresses, this mode of taking alcohol is undoubtedly effective in the short term, and may be compared to the way drugs are used all over the world – and to Stage Three and Stage Four drinking in the Anglo-Saxon region (see previous chapter). In any longer-term sense, however, such a pattern of drinking cannot be other than negative and damaging. "Society must provide other routes to different degrees of ecstasy," insists Swedish government propaganda being supplied to schools in 1977. What the authorities had in mind, though, was not a move towards "positive" social drinking, but the virtual abolition of alcohol. It is understandable how the Northern races, with their long history of abusive spirit-drinking, have got themselves into this predicament. But the abolition of alcohol, as we shall see in Chapter 3, just never seems to work.

The medical benefits.

Few would disagree that alcohol in moderate amounts cheers people up, promotes conviviality and has many beneficial effects on the human organism. The best illustration of the helpful aspects of alcohol is that moderate drinkers live longer than teetotallers. Dr Morris E. Chafetz, Director of the National Institute of Alcohol Abuse and Alcoholism, says that moderate drinking seems to increase longevity and reduce the chances of developing heart disease. Moderate drinkers, he says, live longer and have a lower rate of reported heart attacks than ex-drinkers or abstainers.

Alcohol has many uses in medicine, but in recent years the drug boom has rather pushed alcohol into the shadows. For a moment, though, let us pretend that alcohol had never existed, but a new drug with the same properties as alcohol had just been invented. Dr William Dock once speculated on this theme, giving the new substance the fictitious name of "methylmethanol".

"Let us suppose that methylmethanol, a substance recently synthesized, was found to be completely free of the ill effects, allergic reactions, blood cell damage, and the other hazards associated with nearly all our antibiotics and sedatives. But methylmethanol, in small doses, proved to be a superb tranquillizer; in larger doses, a good sedative; and in even larger doses, an effective anaesthetic agent. Small doses even improved the ability to solve certain kinds of difficult problems in the calculus. In addition, it dilated blood vessels, caused a decrease in the production of the pituitary antidiuretic hormone, and could be used as a readily absorbed body fuel, up to one-third the daily need for calories. It also increased the absorption of fats in patients with intestinal malabsorption and gave better appetites to many sick people.

"We all know what would happen. The sales of all other sedatives and tranquillizers would slump, four-page spreads in medical journals, and neat stories in the papers and news weeklies would make M-M a household name like aspirin. The stock of the patent licensees would go through the ceiling on Wall Street. The lucky discoverer would get every possible honour, as did the men who gave us insulin and hay fever pills. The medical school where the studies were made would found an institute supported by millions in royalties. Humanity would be benefited for untold thousands of years, and the Russians would announce that they had discovered M-M back in Czar Nicholas's day."

Alcohol produces its maximum benefits when used as a food, that is, when consumed as part of a regular meal in not very large amounts. When you take a glass or two of wine or a bottle of beer with your meal, the alcohol contributes to the metabolism much as do fats or carbohydrates, "sparing" the proteins – that is, leaving the proteins to build body tissue and using the alcohol along with fat and carbohydrates to produce energy. Also, the psychological effect of the alcohol, acting as it does as both a mild tranquillizer and euphoriant, helps produce a feeling of well-being. For centuries, alcohol was prescribed routinely as a tonic, and it does have many tonic effects on the body.

Appetite stimulation.
A small amount of alcohol, one drink or two, acts to enhance the appetite, especially if the drink contains very little sugar and at least some bitter or sour-tasting constituents. A true aperitif should not contain more than 20% absolute alcohol. Such fortified wines as sherry or vermouth, or aperitifs like Dubonnet or Campari, are excellent appetite inducers. With a mixed drink, made with hard liquor, there should be considerable dilution of the liquor. In other words, a martini or a manhattan is not quite as appetite-stimulating as something weaker. The stimulating effect from your drink occurs almost instantaneously, but does not last very long, perhaps twenty minutes. You should therefore eat fairly soon after drinking, and drink no more than two true aperitifs or two fairly weak cocktails. If you keep on drinking, the appetite-enhancing effect disappears.

In some cases the addition of alcohol to the diet of people who are weak, run-down or convalescent is often dramatically useful. For instance, a patient recovering from a long, serious illness is uncomfortable, apprehensive, doesn't rest well, and has no appetite. He has lost weight during his ordeal and needs to be built up. He does not seem to absorb sufficient nourishment from his regular diet. He will also tend to be irritable and need sedation every night. Now, if you add alcohol to his diet you may produce a very different picture. From the alcohol the patient is getting a readily available source of calories, which enable him better to utilize the proteins in his diet and so rebuild his depleted organism. The alcohol makes him more cheerful, more relaxed, and the chances are he will no longer need to take a sleeping pill before he gets to sleep. He will begin to gain weight. He will have a better appetite – in short, what might have been a long-drawn-out convalescence is speeded up.

People who don't digest well because they don't produce enough gastric acid can be markedly helped by alcohol, particularly if it's in the form of table wine. Both red and white table wine also contain significant amounts of iron, which is readily absorbed by the organism. The patient with iron-deficiency anaemia who drinks three glasses of table wine per day will get from them 25% or more of his daily iron requirement, which is why wine has been prescribed for anaemia for a century or more.

Alcohol, the heart and the arteries.
There is evidence that alcohol acts in ways not yet completely known to prevent disease in the coronary arteries, and cardiovascular disease. Researchers have repeatedly found that coronary disease is significantly less frequent in countries where wine is part of the everyday diet. Whether or not it is actually a preventive, alcohol is certainly useful in cases where disease involving the heart or arteries does exist. It acts to dilate the peripheral blood vessels, thus reducing the load on the heart, and in addition soothes the tensions and anxieties which usually come along with these ailments. Heart specialists have recognized the value of alcohol for over two centuries. For generations, alcohol was the recognized drug for angina pectoris, for instance, and is still considered by many doctors equal to the now-customary nitrate treatment. The famous cardiologist Paul Dudley White recommended alcohol to many of his patients. Another cardiologist, Irving S. Wright, former president of the American Heart Association, prescribes an ounce or two of whisky every four hours for patients with arteriosclerosis, because "Few, if any, drugs for dilating the arteries are as effective".

Diabetes.
The diabetic, who has to reduce drastically his intake of sugars and carbohydrates, can be particularly benefited by alcohol. As Chauncey Leake says in his book *Alcoholic Beverages in Clinical Medicine:*
"Long before the introduction of insulin in diabetes therapy, and even after insulin became available, alcoholic beverages were customarily prescribed for diabetic patients. Many European clinicians still regularly employed them, dry table wines in particular, as an important part of the diabetic diet, for the physiological as well as the psychological well-being of the subject. In the United States, the use of alcoholic beverages in diabetic therapy fell into temporary disfavor during Prohibition, but, according to Lucia and others, many American physicians have returned to the use of appropriate alcoholic beverages in uncomplicated diabetes with generally satisfactory results. Joslin has reported that in no disease is the employment of alcohol more useful or more justifiable."

Studies have shown that the diabetic can drink as much as 24 oz dry table wine daily with no significant rise in his blood-sugar levels. Psychologically, the freedom to drink can be extremely important for a diabetic because of his restricted and often unpleasurable diet. With severe diabetics, however, many doctors try to forbid alcohol because they're afraid the patient will lose track of time while drinking and forget to take his insulin shots.

A tonic for old age.

Many elderly people tend to be cranky and irritable, or morose and depressed, or withdrawn and despondent. Physicians in charge of nursing homes and homes for the elderly have been finding in recent years that they can prescribe a drink or two rather than the multitude of tranquillizers, mood elevators and sedatives which they formerly employed. In many nursing homes, introducing a cocktail hour has resulted in a dramatic improvement in the general atmosphere. The place begins to seem more like a private house than a hospital, the patients become more gregarious and cheerful, and more civilized and sociable. Introducing liquor gives the patients more dignity and makes them seem more like senior adults than elderly children at the mercy of attendants and doctors. At the Ann Lee Home and Infirmary in Albany, New York, for instance, Dr George A. Cuttita found that when he began serving nightly drinks of brandy to his patients, the number of patients taking tranquillizers dropped from 40% to only 18%.

3. The politics of alcohol.

The sometimes heavy hand of public opinion. Guzzlers and teetotallers. The licensing laws, their origins and how they work today. Women and children — the new "problem drinkers".

It seems to be a requirement of Anglo-Saxon life that we should not enjoy our drinking too much. Outside the home we are obliged by custom, law and convenience to do most of our drinking in places that have been granted a special licence to serve alcohol. By definition there is something clinical about such "dispensaries": like it or not, we must suffer the wish of officialdom to protect us. It is as though the ghosts of Gin Lane are never far away.

Of course, it is in the interests of publicans, clubowners and other licence-holders to keep the ghosts well out of sight, screened by suitably dense facades of "good cheer". Many licencees are mercifully expert at creating good cheer, and we, their customers, are for the most part happy to go along with the conventions involved: we adopt certain pubs as "locals", and generally celebrate their existence as a civilizing influence on our lives. Why, then, does the notion revolve perpetually round our skulls that liquor is evil, and drinking a sin?

To understand present-day attitudes towards alcohol and drinkers, we need to look back some two hundred years to a time when men absorbed enormous quantities of alcohol, and when organized opposition to drinking was first beginning to make itself felt.

In the middle of the 18th century drunkenness was practised, for pleasure and oblivion, at all levels of society. Lady Mary Wortley Montagu wrote that the country squires were "insensible to other pleasures than the bottle and the chase . . . their mornings are spent among the hounds, and their nights with as beastly companions with what liquor they can get." Appetites for meat and drink were huge ("I have drunk three bottles of port without being the worse for it," said Dr Johnson) and were stretched still further in competitive, all-night sessions. Along with the ability to bear physical pain, gamble with fortitude, duel, and carry out bizarre "dares", drinking was a necessary asset for a gentleman. "No, Sir," averred Dr Johnson on another occasion, "claret is the liquor for boys; port for men; but he who aspires to be a hero must drink brandy." The mob, meanwhile, ill-nourished, overworked and uneducated, drank like horses (in the words of a then popular phrase) to anaesthetize its woes as the country slid towards the social devastations of the Industrial Revolution.

In their careless, unbuttoned outlook the better-off Georgians, that is, the ones with the freedom to choose how to pass their days, were carrying on a tradition of heavy drinking that went back centuries to the Middle Ages, when ale was deemed as important as bread and children were discouraged from drinking the unreliable water and were given small beer instead. There had been, however, one important hiccup in the continuity of this tradition. The Puritans, especially under Cromwell, had sought to revolutionize people's attitudes towards eating and drinking by denouncing luxuries such as the spices commonly used in cooking, and by imposing restrictions on lavish or prolonged entertainments; at the same time non-alcoholic beverages like tea and coffee ("slip slops" to their opponents) were permeating the nation. Those who attacked tea as "deleterious produce" had a point, moreover, since anyone giving up his daily ration of small beer to drink tea would be losing a calorific value in the order of 150-200 calories per pint, and replacing it with little more than perfumed water.

When the monarchy was restored in 1660, there was a general reversion to old ways, but the many Puritan-inspired inhibitions were not subdued for long, and, like some monstrous hangover needing several thousand nights to form, they had taken a considerable grip on social life by the end of the 18th century. The rising star of Methodism, with its large working-class following, was an important factor; another was the middle-class bent for seemliness and sobriety in all forms of behaviour. It was thus not a great step for drink to be classified in some over-devout or fanatical minds as evil, the "Devil's brew". The idea of temperance, of going without, became increasingly fashionable, although there was a notable division between those reformers who, like the Methodist leader John Wesley, required his followers to avoid "buying or selling spiritous liquors, or drinking them, unless in cases of extreme necessity", and the more fanatical of the temperance reformers, who would settle for nothing short of total abstinence.

Since the Restoration there had undoubtedly been widespread abuse of alcohol – and on a scale that would be considered highly dangerous today. Between 1690 and 1729, for example, the annual consumption of gin rose from half a million gallons to almost five million. During that time, as G. M. Trevelyan wrote in his *English Social History*, "Parliament deliberately encouraged the consumption of gin by throwing open the distilling trade and placing on spirits far too light a tax. Distilling . . . consumed corn and was therefore good for the landed interest, and so thought the Parliament of landlords." To improve matters, excise charges were levied on the manufacture of spirits (rather than on their retail sale), and retailers were made to take out an annual licence. But it was not until 1828 that Parliament introduced that great legal milestone, the Alehouse Act. In the meantime the abolitionists and the pro-drink lobby fought a lengthy and generally inconclusive campaign.

The Temperance Movement began in the United States in the 1770s, its influence spreading to Britain in the early 1800s, where it had acquired a considerable reputation by the 1820s. Spirits were the target of the first temperance reformers (who continued, interestingly enough, to serve beer in their reading rooms and coffee houses). But for Joseph Livesey, a cheesemonger from Preston, this was inadequate. Dissatisfied with partial abstinence, he signed a pledge in 1832 with six others in which he agreed "to abstain from all liquors of an intoxicating quality, whether ale, porter, wine or ardent spirits, except as medicine".* To Livesey's meetings came reformed drunkards who told of their alcoholic pasts, and it was one of these, Richard Turner, who coined the word "teetotal", as, stuttering in his enthusiasm, he vowed to be "reet down and out t-t-total for ever and ever!" Teetotalism proved an immediately popular doctrine, its extremism forcing people to take sides who might otherwise have remained neutral.

*The medical clause should be seen not so much as a cunning get-out as a reflection on the beliefs of contemporary medical practitioners, who freely advocated alcohol as a stimulant and as a pain-killer.

Livesey's approach to alcohol was certainly radical, if one-sided. For a more balanced view of the pro-anti argument we might quote Charles Dickens, who in *Sketches by Boz* (1836) wrote: *"Gin-drinking is a great vice in England, but wretchedness and dirt are a greater; and until you improve the homes of the poor, or persuade a half-famished wretch not to seek relief in the temporary oblivion of his own misery, with the pittance which, divided among his family, would furnish a morsel of bread for each, gin-shops will increase in number and splendour. If Temperance Societies would suggest an antidote against hunger, filth, and foul air, or could establish dispensaries for the gratuitous distribution of bottles of lethe-water, gin-palaces would be numbered among the things that were."*

The Alehouse Act of 1828 is important not merely because it provided statutory powers where few had existed before, it is also the foundation stone of the licensing laws that, for better or for worse, remain in force today. Previously, the common law had imposed no restrictions on the sale of intoxicating liquors. There had been regulations authorizing people to keep inns, alehouses and victualling houses, but now the conditions binding the licence-holder were much tighter, and the penalties for breaching them severe. Drunkenness and disorderly conduct on the premises were outlawed, that is, the licensee should not permit them (a harsh task in those times); nor was he to allow what the invaluable *Patterson's Licensing Acts* refers to as "unlawful games, or the assembling of persons of notoriously bad character"; he should, moreover, "keep his house closed, except for the reception of travellers, during the hours of Divine Service on Sundays, Christmas Day, and Good Friday". The emphasis on moral factors is noteworthy.

This Act was followed by a Beerhouse Act (1830) which made it possible for householders to sell beer from their homes, provided they obtained a special two-guinea licence from the Excise. Unfortunately, there was an unseemly rush to obtain these licences, followed by a proliferation of beerhouses followed by an upsurge of drunkenness. This had two effects. It persuaded British temperance societies to direct their efforts mainly at limiting the "traffic" in alcohol, in other words to try and make drink harder to obtain, and it brought about a modified Beerhouse Act, introduced in 1834. This new Act drew a distinction between licences to retail beer on the premises and off them (the birth of the off-licence). Other important legislation brought Sunday closing to Wales (1881), and forbade the sale of alcohol to children under 14 "save in quantities not less than one reputed pint, corked and sealed" (1901). The Licensing Act of 1902 gave power "to apprehend a person found drunk and apparently incapable in any highway or other public place, or on any licensed premises. . . A husband or wife of a habitual drunkard might obtain a maintenance or separation order, and a drunken wife might, with her consent, be committed to, and detained in, an inebriate retreat" (Patterson). Other provisions gave some protection to children in the care of drunks, and made it an offence to sell liquor to habitual drunks or to procure it for them.

Temperance societies now flourished in large numbers on both sides of the Atlantic, and their representatives attacked their task as though engaged in a holy crusade. Alcohol was represented as the prime cause of crime, sexual aberration, epilepsy, feeble-mindedness, venereal disease and racial degeneration. Alcohol was said to poison foetuses in the womb, and parents who drank were called murderers of unborn babies. According to Andrew Sinclair in *Era of Excess*, a "favourite trick of temperance lecturers was to drop the contents of an egg into a glass of pure alcohol and tell their audiences that the curdled mass was similar to the effect of liquor on the lining of the human stomach. A similar horror technique was the threat . . . that drunkards might suddenly catch fire and burn to death, breathing out blue flames. The idea that children born in drunkenness would be defective was stressed and documented."

A best-selling health manual, *Dr Gunn's New Family Physician* had this to say about drink:

"Intemperance not only destroys the health, but inflicts ruin upon the innocent and helpless, for it invades the family and social circle and spreads woe and sorrow all around; it cuts down youth in all its vigour, manhood in its strength, and age in its weakness; it breaks the father's heart, bereaves the doting mother, extinguishes natural affection, erases conjugal love, blots out filial attachment, blights parental hope, and brings down mourning age in sorrow to the grave. It produces fevers, feeds rheumatism, nurses the gout, welcomes epidemics, invites disease, imparts pestilence, embraces consumption, cherishes dyspepsia, and encourages apoplexy and paralytic affections. . . Let no man keep company with his wife for the sake of posterity, except when he is sober, for children

usually prove wine-bibbers and drunkards whose parents begat them when drunk."

Like most people who want to change things, the prohibitionists or propagandists of temperance were prepared to fight dirty, loading their speeches and writings with images of terror and, at the same time, presenting their cause in the holiest of lights, inseparable, it might seem, from the finest aspects of patriotism, justice and morality. Then the First World War arrived. By its end, the effective demise of the temperance movement in Britain had been ensured.

Before the outbreak of war, there had been a long and bitter struggle over a Bill to reduce the number of public houses by a third, which ultimately was thrown out by the House of Lords. When war began, the Government, mindful of the excessive drinking that had gone on during the Boer War (1899–1902), introduced the Intoxicating Liquor (Temporary Restriction) Act. By the end of 1914 pubs were closing at 9 or 10pm, and there was a dramatic fall in public drunkenness. Losses of production in munitions factories and ship-building yards were soon being ascribed (with some reason) to alcoholic excesses, and Lloyd George declared, "We are fighting Germany, Austria, and drink, and the greatest of these deadly foes is drink." The next measure was DORA (Defence of the Realm Act), which invested authority over licensing hours and other powers in a Central Liquor Control Board. Soon Britain was gasping under the shortest licensing hours in her history, usually from 12.30pm to 2pm, and in the evening from 6 o'clock to 9 o'clock. By the end of the war the consumption of alcohol had been more than halved, and the number of cases of drunkenness was only a sixth of what it had been in 1914. From that time, the need for prohibition had evaporated, just as the old excesses had drifted away once the alcohol habit had become more difficult to acquire.

In the USA, however, events moved differently. As American involvement in the war increased, so the Government came under mounting pressure to abolish alcohol, which extremists even described as un-American and pro-German. Doctors and pharmacists were responsive to this anti-alcohol pressure. In 1916, *The Pharmacopoeia of the United States* deleted whisky and brandy from its list of standard drugs. A year later, the House of Delegates of the American Medical Association passed a resolution stating that the AMA opposed the use of alcohol as a beverage;

believed there was no scientific basis for its use in therapeutics or as a tonic, stimulant or food; and that the use of alcohol as a therapeutic agent should be discouraged – this despite the fact that in those years a huge majority of the members of the AMA did indeed prescribe alcohol as a therapeutic agent for a wide variety of complaints, and would continue to do so.

As Andrew Sinclair says in *Era of Excess:*

"The resolution was extremely useful to the drys in their campaign for national prohibition. Senator Sterling of South Dakota, referred to it in the debate on the Eighteenth Amendment as "one of the most valuable pieces of evidence we can find in support of the submission of this amendment to the several States of the Union." Wayne B. Wheeler quoted it as definitive evidence while defending the dry definition of "intoxicating" in the courts. The resolution was also very profitable to the doctors. After the passage of the Eighteenth Amendment and the Volstead Act, they were the only people who could issue to their patients whisky, brandy and other strong drinks. Moreover, no patent medicine containing alcohol could be officially sold without a doctor's prescription. By constitutional amendment, the doctors controlled all supplies of beverage alcohol in the United States, except for the hard cider of the farmers and the sacramental wine of the priests."

How "profitable" was it for the doctors? Well, for one year of prohibition, 1928, it was estimated that the doctors of America earned about $40 million by writing prescriptions for whisky.

In 1919, the Eighteenth Amendment, prohibiting the manufacture or sale of alcoholic beverages (except for therapeutic or sacramental purposes) was added to the Constitution. That the amendment did not succeed in eliminating "demon drink" was a great disappointment to most drys, driving some of them to frenzies of hatred toward drinkers. In *Era of Excess*, Andrew Sinclair quotes answers to a prize competition for better ways of enforcing prohibition:

"One woman suggested that liquor law violators should be hung by the tongue beneath an airplane and carried over the United States. Another suggested that the government should distribute poison liquor through the bootleggers; she admitted that several hundred thousand Americans would die, but she thought this cost was worth the proper enforcement of the dry law. Others wanted to deport all aliens, exclude wets from all churches, force bootleggers to go to church every Sunday, forbid drinkers to marry,

torture or whip or brand or sterilize or tattoo drinkers, place offenders in bottle-shaped cages in public squares, make them swallow two ounces of castor oil, and even execute the consumers of alcohol and their posterity to the fourth generation."

America reacts to prohibition

In winning the battle of prohibition, it turned out, the dry forces lost their war – a war to assert the virtues of the countryside over the vices of the city, the righteousness of the native American over the dissolute ways of foreigners and immigrants. Prohibition made drinking glamorous. Where it had been a vice of the working class, drinking now became a badge of sophistication, a mark of wealth and *savoir-faire.* To take a drink was to strike a blow against repression and to assert one's superiority over the repressive, know-nothing class that the journalist H. L. Mencken had christened "the booboisie". Middle-class people who had never before had any interest in drinking hastened to find themselves bootleggers and get introductions to speakeasies. Women, too, began to drink as never before, to the point where, as Heywood Broun commented, a man had to fight his way through crowds of schoolgirls to make his way to the bar.

It was not just drinking that became popular. Urban America became infatuated with almost everything the drys disapproved of: dancing, cigarette smoking, card playing, even (among the more daring souls) the smoking of opium and sniffing of cocaine. This was the age of the Flapper, who smoked, drank, danced the tango and Charleston. Virtually all the celebrities and "opinion leaders" of the 1920s were wets. Jimmy Walker, with his penchant for chorus girls and "black velvets" (champagne and Guinness) became mayor of New York. Authors like John O'Hara and F. Scott Fitzgerald celebrated the hard-drinking ways of the "Jazz Age."

Drunkenness was a badge of manliness for men, of emancipation for women. Almost everybody who was anybody drank. Think of John Barrymore, Sinclair Lewis, Dorothy Parker, Gene Fowler, Wilson Mizner, W. C. Fields . . . Fields' attitudes about liquor were a low-comedy exaggeration of wet opinion. Robert Lewis Taylor tells an illuminating story in *W. C. Fields, His Follies and Fortunes: "Grady was driving the car through the South one night while Fields sat in the back seat on the trunk. The comedian was drinking what he described as "martinis"; he had a bottle of gin in one hand and a bottle of vermouth in the other, and he took alternate pulls, favouring the gin. At an intersection in a country town they saw a man with a satchel making signals under a street lamp. Grady said, 'Fellow wants a ride.'*

'Pick him up,' cried Fields. 'Where's your sense of charity?'

Grady slowed down, called out, 'Hop in the back,' and waited till the man got aboard. As they drove off, Fields extended the bottle of gin to him, but the man refused with a look of offended piety. About five miles down the road, the stranger took some tracts out of his coat pocket and said, 'Brothers, I'm a minister of the gospel.'

Fields blew a mouthful of gin on the floor and the man went on, 'You're sinning in this automobile and though I don't ordinarily do no free preaching, I'm going to preach a free sermon right here.' He examined the tracts and added, 'To tell you the truth, I'm a-going to give you Number Four.'

'What's Number Four?' said Fields.

'Called the Evils of Alcohol,*' said the minister.*

Fields leaned over and said to Grady, 'Pull up beside the first ditch you see.'

The minister's narrative had reached a point where a roustabout had pawned his small daughter's shoes to raise money for a drink when Grady slammed on the brakes.

'Aus! Aus!' Fields began to cry, harking back to his German period, and he kicked the minister into the ditch. Then he opened his trunk, removed an unopened bottle of gin, and tossed it down beside him. 'There's my Number Three,' he yelled. 'Called How to Keep Warm in a Ditch.'

Grady drove on. Fields told him afterwards he'd suspected the minister might be a Methodist. He'd had a lot of trouble with Methodists, he said."

If prohibition was bulldozed into law by crude propaganda tactics, its repeal was brought about, in part, by an even more potent weapon – laughter and ridicule. How could one forever retain a statute that had become a joke? So in 1933, a year of deep Depression, the Twenty-first Amendment superseded the Eighteenth. The newsreels of the day showed great merriment on the occasion, with crowds toasting the cameras in bars, taverns and cocktail lounges (the word "saloon", in deference to the drys, had been made taboo and still remains so). But with the Depression and its unemployment, the nation was anything but merry.

Rise of the doctors.

The years since the 1930s have seen a general upgrading of the medical profession. Christianity by then was losing its broad appeal, and there was no generally recognized authority which could pass judgment on moral or social dilemmas. This gap the medical profession proceeded to fill. In fairness, no takeover conspiracies existed. Despite a certain readiness, the medical profession did not invite the take over. One might call physicians the reluctant priesthood. Throughout the 1930s the public became gradually more infatuated with the doctor-as-hero. Movies like the *Doctor Kildare* series were being turned out by every major studio. Books and novels about medical men were bestsellers. Magazines like the *Reader's Digest* found the profession good copy and turned out hundreds of articles on medical topics. With the help of the AMA's superb public-relations machine, the mystique of the physician as superbeing – kindly, wise and all-knowing, bound to a strict humanitarian code of ethics through his quasi-religious Hippocratic Oath – was widely propagated.

At the same time, the profession was expanding its powers, claiming dominion over vast new territories – mental illness, alcoholism, drug addiction, the control of obesity. The AMA was also winning its battle with its long-time enemy, the patent-medicine industry. Many proprietary medicines were taken off the market, and others were restricted to sale by prescription only, and the manufacturers of the remaining products, in many cases, were forced to include a "commercial" to the medical profession on every package ("If symptoms persist, consult your physician," etc.).

The readiness of the profession to serve as an agent of social control was welcomed by the Government. What a neat solution to the problem of handling the deviant citizens – drunken, disorderly, eccentric or obstreperous persons. Define them as "ill" and turn them over to the doctors for "treatment"! That the treatment in many cases has been ineffective is of little importance; the Government has found it handy to co-opt the medical profession and give it powers over various social problems. Today's physician is an important functionary with much authority over the public at large. He can give them or deny them access to drugs and medication, certify them as insane, alcoholic or drug-addicted, even decide whether to keep them alive or let them die. There is a good deal of truth in the contention of Dr Thomas Szasz (author of *Ceremonial Chemistry, The Myth of Mental Illness,* and other books critical of medical orthodoxy) that we are now living in a "pharmacratic" society.

While some doctors welcome their new powers and responsibilities, others resent them as an imposition, because as the doctors acquired more power, the Government also asserted more control over them. It tells them which modes of treatment they may use and which not, which drugs they may prescribe and which not.

The "official" view of alcohol.

The medical view of alcohol, which is the official one today, attempts to reconcile the broadest possible spectrum of both "wet" and "dry" sentiment. Alcohol is no longer considered evil, but is now a "medically suspect" substance. "Responsible" (moderate) drinking is condoned or even given mild approval while "irresponsible" drinking, which leads to illness or is in itself an illness, is deplored. The irresponsible drinker is himself not to blame, however: he is said to be suffering from an illness that compels him to drink. This kind of medical theology can sometimes seem as foolish as earlier theologies which argued over how many angels could dance on the point of a pin. Dr Szasz quotes from an editorial in *The American Journal of Psychiatry* which noted approvingly that the "public image" of the alcoholic has been changed successfully from that of a "skid-row derelict to that of a worthwhile person suffering from an illness which can be successfully arrested so that he (or she) can take his rightful place in society – a good parent, good spouse, good neighbor, good worker, and a productive citizen with a social conscience." Dr Szasz goes on to comment:

"I doubt that any leading medical journal would assert, in equally sweeping terms, that patients suffering from diabetes, hypertension, or tuberculosis, are, one and all, 'worthwhile persons'. What, I should like to know, makes the alcoholic – any alcoholic, according to the quotation cited – a 'worthwhile person'? If alcoholism is a disease, like other diseases, how can it impart moral value to the person who has it? If having a disease does not make an individual worthless, it also cannot make him worthwhile! To my mind, an individual is a worthwhile or worthless human being – depending on what he does or does not do with his life – whether he has diabetes, heart trouble, or the habit of drinking too much.

If alcoholism is a disease, why do we need propagandists and politicians to tell us so? We neither need nor use laymen to tell us that cancer and heart disease are illnesses. Why, then, do we need President Johnson to proclaim that 'The alcoholic suffers from a disease which will yield eventually to scientific research and adequate treatment'?"

Myth or not (we'll examine that question in a subsequent chapter), the idea that "irresponsible" drinking is an illness called alcoholism in an integral part of the official view of alcohol.

The new "problem drinkers"

In Britain the notion of the "caring society" is securely entrenched. It is as well, since post-war prosperity has brought with it the customary rise in excessive drinking. (This is nothing new; there is plenty of historical evidence to show that affluence increases the consumption of alcohol; it happened frequently during the nineteenth century as levels of prosperity rose and fell, and no doubt it will continue to happen – though in the present Age of the Consumer the falls tend to be smaller than the rises.)

Facilities for looking after "problem drinkers" are now being set up in most major towns, and a number of hospitals have specialist alcohol units. However, the sheer number of people with drink problems, coupled with a general shortage of money to spend on them, is causing dismay. Another reason not to feel complacent is that two new kinds of "problem drinkers" have recently been identified – women and young people. There is no doubt that Britons are now drinking appreciably more than a few years ago, and that they are starting younger. A Glasgow survey of "Teenagers and Alcohol" indicated that 85% of girls and 92% of boys had drunk alcohol before the age of 14.

"Beer not Glue" reads an aerosol graffito on a London Underground station. The sign marks a significant move among the young away from drug abuse, from pill-popping upwards, and into drinking. Alcohol is now very easy to obtain at virtually any hour of the day until late in the evening, either in pubs, or off-licences, or in supermarkets, and this new super-availability has coincided with a marked rise in drunkenness amongst the young that is currently estimated to be increasing at about 10% per year.

Among the previous generation of young, that is, those who were actively experimenting with drugs in the 1960s, alcohol has also returned to favour. Partly this is probably a matter of convenience: as people mature and their domestic situations become more stable, so alcohol may be more favoured simply because it is easier to obtain than drugs. At the same time there has been a slight resurgence of the cocktail among, principally, the same age group. The cocktail remains in most minds an emblem of 1920s elegance; but the general flavour of the 1970s is one of high informality, of fashionable scruffiness, and the new interest shown in cocktails is perhaps more important for indicating a renewal of interest in the kind of sensory experiments that in the 1960s the Beautiful Young were conducting with drugs. The essence of a cocktail, after all, is that it is strong, and gets into the system fast. Two or three are all you need for an alcoholic high.

The problem of women drinkers is more serious. They, with school-age teenagers, represent the new growth areas in excessive and uncontrolled drinking. The "women" are, typically, housewives marooned at home all day while their husbands are out working, and who relieve their boredom and tensions by drinking. Their drinking almost invariably gets worse, since the fact that they keep a bottle in the wardrobe doesn't make them less lonely. They remain bored and isolated, their drink problem compounded by the fact that relatively little is known about them. They are one of several kinds of secretive drinker, usually too ashamed or afraid to come out and declare themselves. As a social category they are enigmatic; but it is fairly certain that their numbers are on the increase.

In 1976, the number of women found guilty of drunkenness (8,642) was 14% higher than the 1975 figure. In the same period the number of men convicted, though much larger at 100,056, reflected an annual rise of only 3%. While these figures may be interpreted in a variety of ways, they and their like have helped to apply pressure on the Government to try and increase public awareness of the problems induced by excessive drinking.

The character of the late 1970s in Britain has been heavily marked by the economic recession that began in 1973. In terms of resources to cope with "problem drinkers", there is not enough money to go round, and the available services are under considerable strain. Ironically, while society has become vastly more tolerant of drinking and its victims, and the liquor industry flourishes as never before, far too little is being spent on the environmental and other causes of alcoholism, and on caring for the known sick. If all the new "problem drinkers" were suddenly to make themselves known and ask for help, it is unlikely that much could be done for them.

However, at the beginning of 1978 the Government spokesmen, fortified by the prospect of North Sea oil revenues, were becoming insistent in their talk of economic recovery, and fresh initiatives were launched in the battle against the misuse of alcohol. Meanwhile the mass of the drinking population found it as difficult as ever to perceive any tangible benefits in the heralded economic turnabout, and suspicions were voiced that this Whitehall-inspired "mini-miracle" was an impalpable thing, the sort of airy material usually associated with an election year.

Initiatives were nevertheless taken that may provoke a radical rethink of public attitudes towards alcohol. For the first time since the Great War, alcohol was being publicly isolated and examined not just as a substance abused by an unfortunate minority but as a much more dangerous commodity that can and does undermine the health of millions of people. As such, drinking was being aligned with smoking, and the Department of Health announced that it would be publishing a consultative document later in the year in which many possible future forms of legislation would be mooted. These would include the banning of all drink advertising, and the addition to all drink labels of a "Government Health Warning", such as cigarette packets already carry.

The Advertising Standards Authority has also been trying to formulate a new code of practice for drink advertising. At present spirits are not openly advertised on TV, and there has been criticism of supermarkets which include their hard-liquor sections in across-the-board advertisements. One early target is likely to be the fortified wines group – the Martini-Cinzano-Noilly Prat set – which unrelentingly solicits custom by associating its products with expensive available girls, glamorous locations and the kinds of fun that only the upper-income crust takes for granted.

The British can therefore look forward to various forms of tightening-up, both in legislation and in education, since it appears that the Government intends to spend money on preventing harmful drinking as well as curing the victims of it. A recent campaign in the North-East was essentially educational, and was beamed via TV, local radio, posters, etc., at the young drinker. Moderation, though, is an elusive goal, and it will very probably take a generation or more to convince people of the need to scale down, and in some cases cut out altogether, something that has become an automatic social habit.

The British are even less likely to welcome pressures from abroad to moderate their use of alcohol. But recent noises emanating from the Brussels home of the EEC dinosaur suggest that moves are afoot to harmonize official policies in the Community towards drink, beginning with the formulation of a common code of advertising practice. These proposals will undoubtedly hit troubled waters, if not terminal rocks, since they involve cutting across the entrenched social customs of widely differing cultures. As we discussed in the section on National Attitudes in Chapter 2, a Briton, a Frenchman and a German prefer different kinds of drink, and typically consume them at different times of day and at different rates. Since, too, the French and the Germans are considered to have significantly worse drink problems than the other member nations, it is hard to see how any common code of practice can be either acceptable to all, or properly effective.

The drink industry meanwhile continues to play its customary Janus game of facing simultaneously in opposite directions. On the one side the brewers and distillers have a responsibility to their shareholders to improve their profits each year, which even allowing for inflation and internal efficiency is unlikely to happen without a corresponding increase in the volume of sales. To satisfy these commercially sensible urges, the general public must therefore be persuaded to drink more. This Janus face might be portrayed à la Gillray with eager staring eyes, full-lipped open mouth and lolling, clearly parched tongue.

The other face is tight-lipped and severe, as befits the custodian and manufacturer of dangerous fluids. This sector acts as the conscience of the organism. Among its activities it supervises the issue of booklets to its salesmen telling them how to comport themselves while touring the company's retail outlets, occasionally restrains the stark aggression of its advertising campaigns, and gives money to foundations seeking to combat alcoholism.

In these various deeds can be detected a degree of hypocrisy. It is discernible, too, that the brewers and distillers prefer to see their money spent on the clinical treatment of people in the final phase of their alcoholic careers, when it might be better spent alerting the young to the dangers of alcohol. That, however, may change as the effects begin to be felt of the Government's recent swing towards investing in prevention rather than cure as the sounder long-term policy.

Part two. The trouble with drinking.

4. It gives you hangovers.

The head aches, the stomach is queasy, the limbs feel barely able to drag you around . . . you're hung over. What is a hangover, why do we get them, how can we cure or prevent them?

Some drinkers experience no hangover at all after a night of unusually heavy drinking. Others have only a mildly "not-quite-up-to-par" feeling. Still others experience excruciating torment. The symptoms of hangover vary from individual to individual, and they vary, also, according to how much you drink and how many years you've been drinking. A Finnish investigator, E. Tuominen, says that in early alcoholism, headaches, general indisposition and vomiting are the main hangover symptoms. Moderately advanced alcoholics exhibit tension, irritability, restlessness, stomach disturbances and guilt feelings. In long-standing, severe alcoholism, it is likely that cardiac disturbances and psychotic symptoms will be present. But what are the symptoms of hangover in the normal, non-alcoholic drinker? A Danish study lists 20:

Vomiting,	Headache,
Loss of appetite,	Fatigue,
Heartburn,	Sweating,
Lassitude,	Disturbed balance and gait,
Continued thirst,	Tremor,
Palpitation,	Nystagmus (tremor of the eye-balls),
Weakness of joints,	General malaise,
Respiratory difficulties,	Anxiety,
Sleeplessness,	Depression,
Giddiness,	Pallor.

Basically, the hangover is a bunch of different reactions to the experience of having drunk "too much". Just what constitutes too much depends on the individual drinker. Of the people I interviewed, quantities of alcohol that would produce a hangover varied from "more than two glasses of wine" to "more than a bottle of whisky". If averages mean anything, the average amount that is "too much" seems to be, for heavy drinkers, more than half a bottle of spirits and for more moderate drinkers, more than five or six drinks, during an evening's drinking.

Part of the cause of hangover is that some of the "too much" alcohol from the previous night is still swimming around in your veins the next morning. We drink more than we can oxidize during our night's sleep and wake up still partially drunk. Apparently, heavy drinkers can tolerate some blood alcohol the next day. They can cope with drinking a bottle of spirits, which at the rate of ½ oz of alcohol per hour will take about 12 hours to leave the body, but a bottle and a half (about 18 hours' worth) produces hangover, a hangover that may just conveniently lift in time for the drinker to start his next drinking bout. Since moderate drinkers have hangovers on only six or eight hours' worth of alcohol, however, leftover alcohol is obviously not a cause of all hangovers. Let's look at some other factors.

Fatigue.

Fatigue or lassitude in some form is part of every hangover. Frequently this is the effect of insufficient sleep: if you drink until 2 or 3am and then get up at 7.30 you can't expect to be in tiptop shape. But equally important is the quality of sleep you get. In recent years, studies of sleep have shown that there is a type of sleep called REM (rapid eye movement) sleep which is particularly important to the mental and physical well-being of the sleeper. When deprived of REM sleep, experimental subjects became irritable and anxious. Since in REM sleep the cortex or higher brain is very active, persons whose cortexes have been anaesthetized by alcohol or sleeping pills cannot have REM sleep until the anaesthesia wears off. So, if you go to bed sodden, the sleep you get for the next few hours will be unrestful and unrefreshing.

Another type of fatigue is due to the direct physiological effects of alcohol. We have seen how alcohol numbs the higher brain, masking its awareness of minor pain, fatigue or malaise. Failing to receive any signs of stress, the brain allows the body to over-exert (the phrase "roaring drunk" conjures up the extreme phase of alcoholic over-exertion). Even if the drinker does not stay out all night, dancing or roaring about, his central nervous system is still out of control, allowing heartbeat, respiration and other functions to speed up without check. This over-exertion produces a fatigue that is not felt at the time but is painfully obvious when the cortex wakes up.

Headache.

The causes of the morning-after headache are not fully known. Perhaps there is not just one hangover headache. One type could be due to vasodilation, enlargement of the sensitive cranial arteries. Alcohol is a vasodilator, but since the headache does not occur at the time when alcohol is at a high level in the bloodstream, it is not directly caused by the alcohol but by fatigue, dehydration and other factors. Another kind of headache is the muscle-contraction or "tension" headache. This could be produced by sleeping with your head in an awkward posture for many hours. Allergy headaches could be produced by a sensitivity to the congeners in straight whisky, or to substances such as tyramine – a central-nervous-system stimulant present in port, sherry and red table wines – or histamine, a vasodilator contained in significant amounts in certain red wines, particularly Burgundies.

Caffeine, a vasoconstrictor, may help ease a headache due to vasodilation (hence the fame of black coffee as a cure, or at least a partial cure). Aspirin, a muscle relaxant, will subdue the tension headache. Take some of both, drink plenty of fluids, and, if you can, go back to bed and get some more sleep. Probably your headache is allied to a shortage of sleep, and, as the level of alcohol in your system subsides, so you can expect the quality of your sleep to improve (more REM, which is what you particularly need to lift you out of your present discomfort).

Most moderate social drinkers will have heard the next well-worn piece of advice many times before, but for as long as people ignore it, or "forget", it is worth repeating that your morning-after headache could well have been avoided by taking something *before* you went to bed. Nearly all drinkers have a good enough idea of their capacity for alcohol to judge whether there is a likelihood of "trouble" the next day. If there is, the obvious thing is to counter it straight away by taking some familiar remedy that can go to work while you are asleep.

Even on those occasions when the "sober you" has been overwhelmed by the "drunk you", and all you feel capable of is flopping out in a chair or crawling heavily into bed, all need not be lost. Get someone to help you. Most people live with at least one other person, and it should be possible for her, him or them to make sure you take at least your regular hangover precautions before you go to sleep for the night. And if you live alone, maybe there is a sympathetic neighbour who will look after you. You can always ask – preferably beforehand on the first occasion. Maybe you'll find yourself arranging some rota of mutual support of the "You Friday, me Saturday" kind. It should be a relatively simple matter of communication – well worth a try, anyhow. If it's not so simple, or worse still, you can't talk reasonably about your drinking sessions with your wife/lover/neighbour, it's time you switched from thinking about short-term hangover cures and looked more closely into the reasons why you are drinking too much.

Alcoholic "dehydration".

The extreme thirst sometimes felt during hangover is not caused by any real depletion of body fluids. True, alcohol does cause increased urination, but this is not sufficient to make for any significant drying-out of the body. What causes thirst is that the alcohol acts to alter the distribution of water in the body. Normally, about two-thirds of the water in the body is held within the cells. Alcohol causes this balance to change, decreasing the amount of fluid in the cells and increasing extra-cellular fluids. The body as a whole has lost no water, but the cells are feeling parched; hence your thirst.

Nausea, vomiting, heartburn.

Drinking too much strong liquor is a shock (or "insult", as some doctors like to call it) to the digestive system. For a neophyte drinker, two or three drinks are sufficient insult to cause his stomach to rebel. A fairly experienced drinker may require a great deal more to bring him to the same state. The habitual heavy drinker's stomach, like the old dray horse that has become inured to the whip, has learned that it's useless to try to fight off the booze and so does not. Vomiting during or right after drinking usually occurs only with relatively inexperienced or non-tolerant drinkers.

Morning-after vomiting, however, can happen to the most habituated. The digestive system was able to cope with the overload of liquor it was given the previous night, but now it rejects any further contributions. The hungover drinker swallows his breakfast orange juice and suddenly it's as if he had swallowed a depth charge. The stomach rumbles and erupts, and will accept no more nourishment until many hours have passed. Finally the crisis passes and digestion is back to normal – until the next overload. Alcoholic irritation of the mucous lining of the digestive tract ("heartburn") is often present, and in some drinkers becomes chronic, so that vomiting and discomfort are frequent. This is a serious problem in that the sufferer tends no longer to eat well; the resulting nutritional deficiencies further aggravate the gastritis and also impair the digestive process so that vitamins and other nutrients are poorly absorbed. At this point a sojourn on the wagon is indicated plus, probably, a supplementary diet of B vitamins. Chronic gastritis should be treated by a physician.

Remorse and emotional pain.

The most excruciating hangover seems to be the one in which the sufferer wakes up and thinks something like, "Oh, I've done it again! I got drunk last night and now I'm being punished. What a miserable, rotten wretch I am!" This phenomenon is common in alcoholics. As Dr Benjamin Karpman says in his book *The Hangover*, "The increasing misery of the hangover is not due to the headache, the nausea, the cold sweats, the chills and fever, or even the shakes, but to the emotional pain that accompanies them – the guilt, anxiety, self-accusation, the sense of hopelessness and despair." These feelings occur with social drinkers too. We probably all know at least one drinker who goes through a hangover doubled over in misery and swearing never, never, never to drink that much again.

One friend of mine who was drinking rather heavily and coming to work late, hungover and remorseful every morning, got fired from his job. "I didn't so much mind his coming in late," his boss reported. "What I couldn't stand were those constant apologies."

Perhaps some of these drinkers are over-dramatizing the whole ritual of drinking and take perverse pride in how drunk they get at night and how terribly they suffer the next morning. Others may have genuine emotional conflicts about drinking (or their behaviour while drinking) which cause them to amplify the pain signals of hangover as a sort of punishment or atonement. Another group may be suffering emotionally because of vitamin depletion. In any case, the worst hangover is the one in which emotional distress predominates.

Is there a hangover cure?

Unfortunately, the hangover has not been the subject of much medical research. Delirium tremens, which might be considered a super-hangover, responds nicely to adrenal steroids, but using such powerful medication on the ordinary hangover would be totally unsound – no doctor would prescribe it.

One possible hangover cure (or preventive) has been identified, but it is not at present available in the UK. The substance in question contains pyritinol and is marketed under the trade name Encephabol. It is manufactured by E. Merck & Co., Darmstadt, West Germany. It is related to but not chemically the same as vitamin B6, pyridoxine.

A number of studies had indicated that Encephabol had a protective effect in animals against the symptoms of alcohol intoxication, and a group of Danish researchers decided to try the substance in experiments with humans. Using a group of volunteers, they made a "double-blind" experiment in which the participants were invited to a series of parties where they were encouraged to drink, talk, sing and dance. One half of the group were given placebos, the other half 1,200 mg of Encephabol in three doses: 400 mg at the beginning of the party, 400 three hours later, and 400 at the end of the party. The next morning the subjects were visited at their places of work, given a checklist of hangover symptoms, and asked to mark those symptoms, if any, they thought were most applicable to their condition. At a subsequent party the roles were reversed: subjects who had received Encephabol received placebos, and vice versa.

The results of the experiment were highly significant. The subjects not receiving Encephabol reported over 50% more hangover symptoms than those who did get the drug. In addition, three participants, after placebo, had total amnesia about what happened at the party, whereas after Encephabol they had no such experience. Some of the subjects who drank the most during the parties exhibited slurred speech during the placebo session but not with Encephabol. The drug is not at present licensed by the American Food and Drug Administration, and no US studies have been made. One would hope, however, that such a promising initial report would be followed up by somebody.

In the UK the drug is also not licensed, but Merck's British company place its use in the treatment of alcohol-induced illnesses low in their priorities. As at the end of 1977, their clinical trials show that while the drug can "enhance cerebral metabolism", they see it being more useful in helping cerebral illnesses of the "failed intellect" kind, and in rehabilitation programmes, for example in treating someone who has suffered a stroke. It appears, too, that licensing standards for new drugs are less stringent on the Continent than they are in the USA and the UK. However, in due time it is possible that clinical trials may be held here to ascertain the possible benefits of Encephabol in the context of alcohol.

How about a hair of the dog that bit you?

Alcohol works tolerably well as a temporary abater of hangovers. If you drink enough to reach Stage One or Stage Two, you may succeed in masking your fatigue and some other minor symptoms. (Taking the booze in a Bloody Mary or other highly spiced drink will help mask gastric distress, much as liniment masks muscle aches.) But in so doing you may not get the rest you need and may find, particularly if you slide into Stage Three or beyond, that next day's hangover is even worse. If you must fight booze with booze, do so only occasionally. Habitual use of more drink to cure hangovers could put you in the same bind as the terminal drunk: he must drink, because only alcohol can make him feel better.

Vitamins can help . . . a little.

Since vitamin deficiencies play so enormous a part in what goes wrong with drinkers, one might expect that taking vitamins would help a hangover. And so it does, for some people. The vitamins most likely to help are the water-soluble ones, B-complex and C, and the minerals. Fat-soluble vitamins such as A, D and E may also be efficient, but there's little chance that taking them would have any results during the period of the hangover, since they go to work more slowly.

A couple of years ago, for instance, I was having severe hangovers – no headache or nausea, but pronounced fatigue plus a highly unsettling internal queasiness or shakiness. I decided to experiment with vitamins and see if I could relieve my symptoms. I began with the B vitamins, taking a high-potency B-complex capsule plus large extra doses of B1, B2, B6, and nicotinamide. Though I could feel, taste, and smell surplus B vitamins exuding from every pore, my hangover remained the same. Then I tried vitamin C – about 2,000 milligrams disolved in water. There was an immediate result, but not an especially dramatic one: I felt somewhat refreshed and less worn out though the hangover was still unpleasant. The mitigating effects of the C alone were minimal, however. Then one day it occurred to me I might be deficient in magnesium. Magnesium deficiency can cause nervous and muscular irritability, muscle cramps and spasms, convulsions, and probably is an important factor in causing delirium tremens. I took a teaspoon of Epsom salts (magnesium sulphate) dissolved in water and got almost immediate relief from the queasy, shaky feelings that had been bothering me. I've had hangovers since but never severe ones.*

Other people have reported to me that their hangovers are helped by B vitamins – B1, nicotinamide, and B6 in particular. The point is that for vitamins to be of any effect there must be a deficiency. If you're already a health-food-and-vitamin "true believer", you're probably wasting time and money trying to cure your hangovers with more vitamins.

The only sure cure for hangovers is the traditional one: drink plenty of fluids; eat bland, soothing foods; get lots of rest . . . and be patient!

Preventing the hangover.

It's a lot easier to avoid a hangover than it is to cure one. Here's one system for avoiding hangovers that should be reliable provided you're able to follow *all* the suggestions.

1. Eat before drinking, preferably rather fatty foods. Alcohol has an affinity with fat, and fat retards alcohol absorption more than other foods.
2. Drink less, if you possibly can.
3. After drinking, don't go to sleep straightaway. Stay up for two or more hours. Drink lots of fluids, have a few cups of coffee, eat something. If you're headachy, take two aspirin before going to bed.
4. Sleep late.
5. Be complacent, rather than guilty, about your drinking.

*Proprietary brands such as Andrews Liver Salt and Alka-Seltzer are widely used by British drinkers, often in tandem with aspirin, in the belief that "one is for the gut, the other for the head".

5. It can make you fat.

Drinking can quickly dig into your calorie quota, making you heavier than you should be. Work out how many calories you need, and balance your intake of food and alcohol. And take more exercise.

A drinker would seem to have two choices: eat a normal diet and get fat, or cut his food intake and be malnourished. Of the two, the first choice seems preferable, particularly if one's drinking tends to be heavy rather than light. A thin person lives on a tight metabolic budget and easily depletes his reserves of energy and nutriments. Heavy drinking is much more apt to disturb him than it will a fleshier person. Of the thirty-five or so heavy drinkers I interviewed, only six were decidedly thin, and four of these seemed to have more than their share of alcoholic problems: inability to "handle" liquor, with frequent descents into Stage Three and Stage Four while the rest of the crowd was enjoying itself; hangover symptoms that sounded like incipient polyneuritis; blackouts and minor accidents that happened more often than with heftier drinkers. Heavy drinking, after all, is a sort of gastro-intestinal athleticism. The typical alcoholic athlete tends to be tubby, like a Sumo wrestler, or at least on the fleshy side of "normal" for his height and frame. It is one of the occupational hazards of working in the drink industry: just think of the publicans you know; the majority, almost certainly, will be overweight.

Is it possible, though, to drink, remain healthy, and yet be slim? Yes, but the difficulty of doing so is directly proportionate to the amount you drink. On two whiskies a day, you're adding about 120 calories to your intake, two pints of beer, about 360 calories . . . four whiskies, 240 calories, four pints of beer, 720 calories . . . a bottle of whisky, about 1,600 calories. Obviously, only extraordinary measures can keep down the weight of a bottle-a-day person.

Working out your calorie surplus.

Do you have an extra-calorie problem, and if so, how large is it? To find out, we need to determine how many of the calories you consume are actually surplus. This is done by comparing your daily calorie requirement with the number of calories you actually consume.

Finding the calorie requirement. A reasonably accurate method of determining how many calories you need is to multiply your body weight by 15. (A 160-pound man of average height and build needs about 160 x 15 or 2,400 calories daily.) The 15-calories-per-pound-of-body-weight figure applies to everyone whose energy expenditures are in the sedentary to moderately-active range. If you spend your working day doing a job involving physical labour (hod carrying, say, or road mending, or carpentry) you may need 20 to 25 calories per pound, depending on how strenuous and prolonged your exertions are.

Average food intake. Count up the food calories you consume. On pages 68-71 is a somewhat abbreviated calorie chart. (More complete ones are available in booklet form in most bookshops.) Add up the calorie values for everything you eat over a 24-hour period. Don't forget the butter on your bread, the sugar in your coffee, all stray snacks and titbits. (If you don't trust your memory to reconstruct your food intake, keep a diary for a day or two, listing everything you eat.)

Alcohol calories. Now count up how much you drink on the average. Find the calorific value from the list on pages 74-75.

Your surplus, if any. Add up your food and liquor count and subtract from it your daily calorie requirement to obtain the amount of the surplus. For instance, let's take a 160-pound man (calorie requirement 2,400) who consumes an average of 2,160 food calories plus three pints of beer and three whiskies (814 calories) daily.

Actual calories	2,160
	814
Total calories	2,974
Minus calorie requirement	2,400
Surplus	574

Since it takes approximately 3,500 calories to add a pound of fat to the body, this man will tend to gain a little over a pound a week on his present diet.

Coping with surplus calories.

There are three basic ways of eliminating or neutralizing a surplus:
1. Cut down on food.
2. Cut down on liquor.
3. Burn up the surplus through exercise.

Let's begin with the last of these.

Exercise.

Are you sedentary? Do you, in other words, spend your working days sitting at a desk, use a car to run errands with, have a houseful of electrical gadgets to do your chores for you? If so, exercise is the most important form of weight control you could possibly undertake.

The sedentary life is physiologically abnormal for both humans and animals. In his book *Overweight*, Dr Jean Mayer, one of the world's foremost authorities on obesity and weight control says: *"That an increase in appetite follows an increase in activity in a normal animal or person is true enough. It explains why the weight of most adults is relatively constant. A fine adjustment of appetite prevents the body from burning away its substance when the individual is called upon to perform at a higher level of exertion than has been his custom. This adjustment of calorific intake to calorific expenditure admits of definite limitations even in a normal person. Energy expenditure must not be raised above a certain upper limit; it must not be lowered beyond a certain minimal limit."*

In the sedentary person, the correlation between physical exertion and appetite has been lost. Sedentary individuals eat more, not less than those who are "normally" active, and since they have no way to burn off the extra calories, they get fat. For an active person, there is a "cost" to becoming overweight – if he gains a few pounds, he will have to burn up extra calories to carry the increased weight through his usual activities. The sedentary individual, however, will expend much less energy in moving his extra weight around; his weight gain will therefore be much more rapid. As Dr Mayer says:

Calorie Counter.

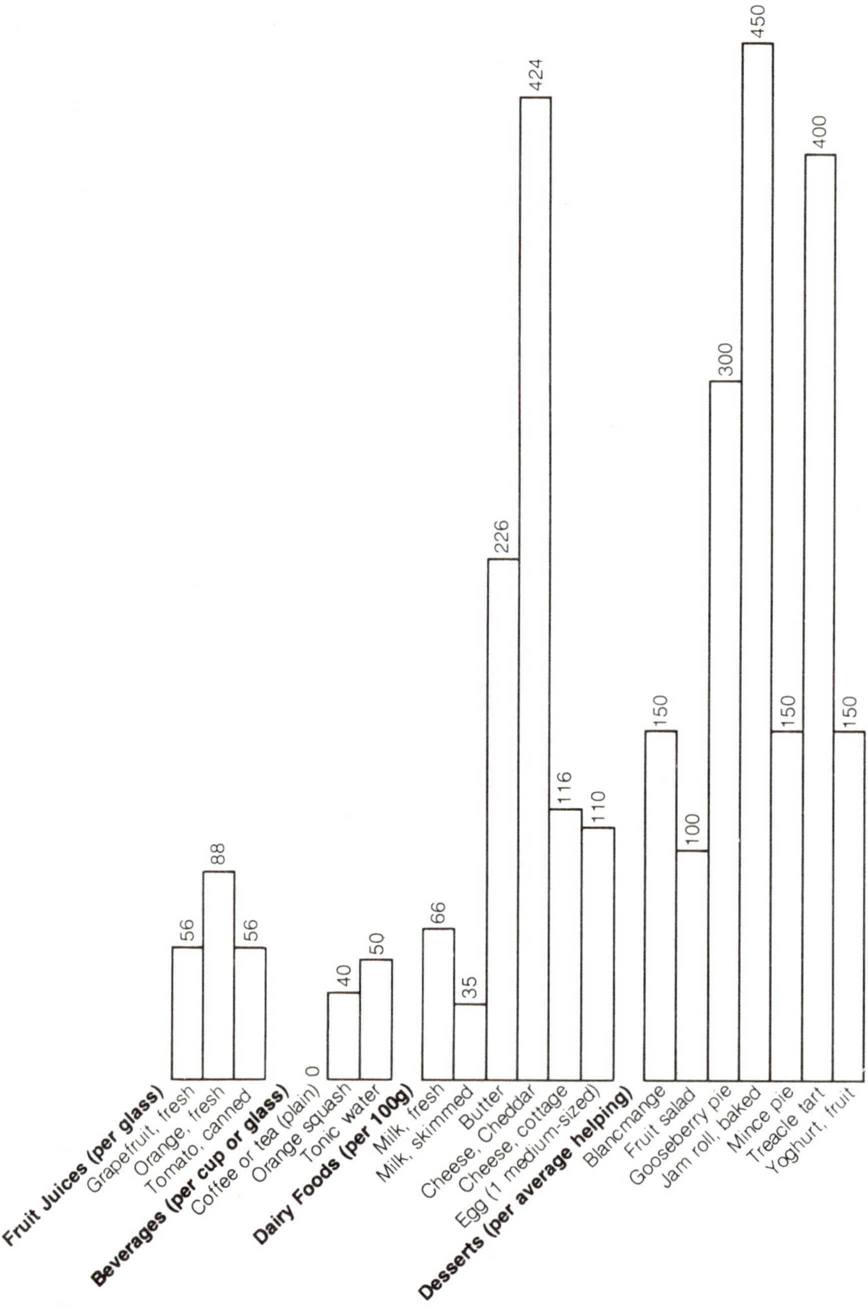

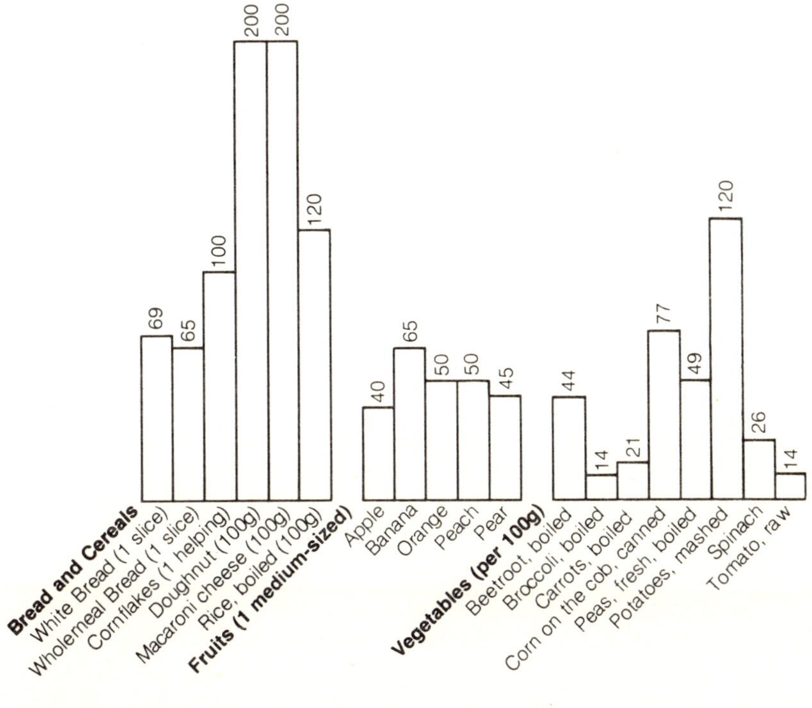
69
65
100
200
200
120
40
65
50
50
45
44
14
21
77
49
120
26
14
Bread and Cereals
White Bread (1 slice)
Wholemeal Bread (1 slice)
Cornflakes (1 helping)
Doughnut (100g)
Macaroni cheese (100g)
Rice, boiled (100g)
Fruits (1 medium-sized)
Apple
Banana
Orange
Peach
Pear
Vegetables (per 100g)
Beetroot, boiled
Broccoli, boiled
Carrots, boiled
Corn on the cob, canned
Peas, fresh, boiled
Potatoes, mashed
Spinach
Tomato, raw

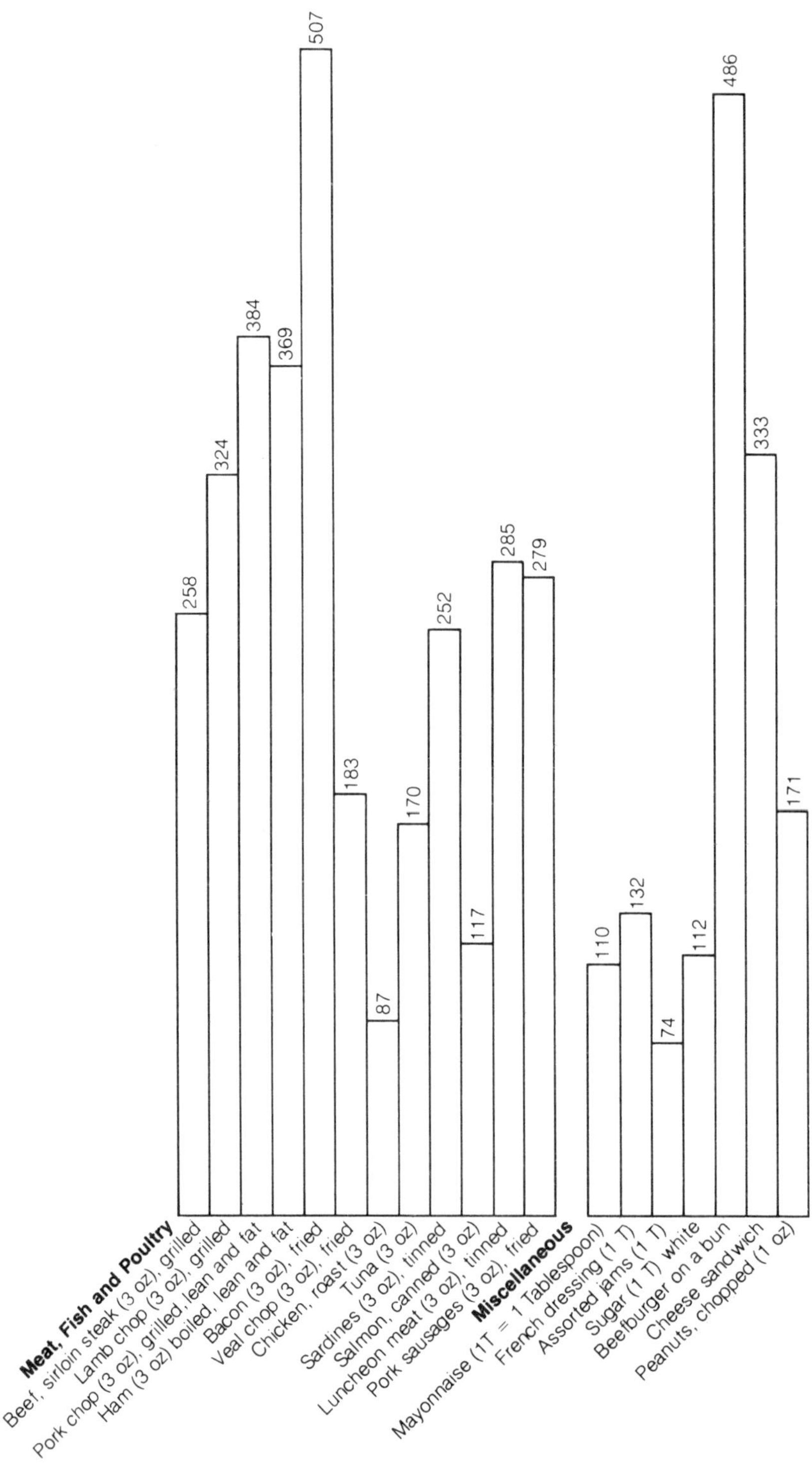

Meat, Fish and Poultry
Beef, sirloin steak (3 oz), grilled
258
Lamb chop (3 oz), grilled
324
Pork chop (3 oz), grilled, lean and fat
384
Ham (3 oz) boiled, lean and fat
369
Bacon (3 oz), fried
507
Veal chop (3 oz), fried
183
Chicken, roast (3 oz)
87
Tuna (3 oz)
170
Sardines (3 oz), tinned
252
Salmon, canned (3 oz)
117
Luncheon meat (3 oz), tinned
285
Pork sausages (3 oz), fried
279
Miscellaneous
Mayonnaise (1T = 1 Tablespoon)
110
French dressing (1 T)
132
Assorted jams (1 T)
74
Sugar (1 T) white
112
Beefburger on a bun
486
Cheese sandwich
333
Peanuts, chopped (1 oz)
171

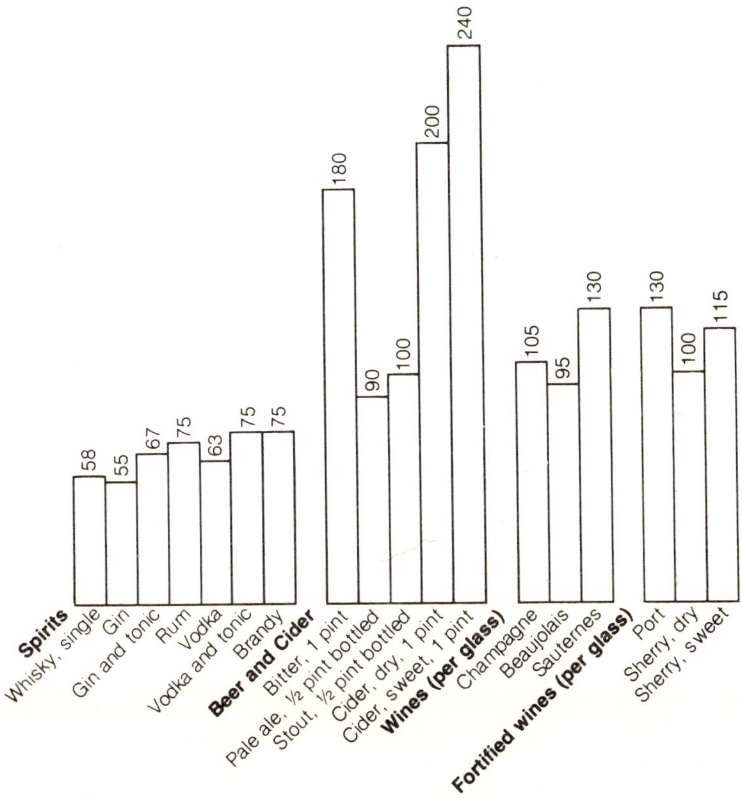

Spirits
Whisky, single
Gin
Gin and tonic
Rum
Vodka
Vodka and tonic
Brandy
Beer and Cider
Bitter, 1 pint
Pale ale, ½ pint bottled
Stout, ½ pint bottled
Cider, dry, 1 pint
Cider, sweet, 1 pint
Wines (per glass)
Champagne
Beaujolais
Sauternes
Fortified wines (per glass)
Port
Sherry, dry
Sherry, sweet
58
55
67
75
63
75
75
180
90
100
200
240
105
95
130
130
100
115

"We . . . sleep all night in comfortable beds, ride to work, sit all day in front of our desks, or stand before our work benches. We ride back home, sit before the dinner table, sit to read our papers and magazines, sit at a motion picture or in front of our television set – and so to bed. We are using our bodies and their marvellous regulatory mechanisms in a way for which they were never designed. Small wonder that, living thus on the fat of the land, many of us become fat. The wonder is that, for many others, appetite does not adjust to this extraordinary set of circumstances."

A sedentary person is an unhealthy person. It's not just that he's apt to be flabby and overweight. He's weak, physically clumsy and inept, less resistant to disease and infection. Less resistant, also, to the effects of toxins such as alcohol and tobacco. A sedentary individual who smokes and drinks heavily runs the risk of taking many more years off his life than an active individual with the same vices. Even disregarding the increased mortality rate, sedentariness is sad because it culminates in a sort of living death. We're all familiar with people in their fifties and sixties who have ceased being viable physical organisms – to them, getting up out of a chair, climbing a flight of stairs, getting in or out of a car are arduous if not semi-impossible activities.

The sedentary person is particularly prone to heart disease. As Dr Laurence E. Morehouse says in his book *Total Fitness:*

"When a sedentary person becomes fairly active by adding a mild exercise such as walking, many changes take place in his body that can be inferred to be important in developing his resistance to cardiac disease. Blood pressure is lowered, resting heart rate decreases, muscles – including the heart muscle – become stronger, there is a vast increase in the number of active small blood vessels which carry blood to the cells of the muscular tissues. The blood itself is improved; it carries more oxygen, and the blood platelets, which become sticky and plug up vessels in the heart and brain, thereby causing heart attacks and strokes, become less sticky with exercise training."

Becoming unsedentary. Any activity involving more than his usual exertion will improve the condition of a sedentary person: walking up and down stairs rather than using the lift, walking or bicycling to the shops rather than driving there in a car, mowing the lawn or pottering in the garden, carrying something heavy, sawing wood, dancing, swimming, playing ping pong . . . the list is endless.

Walking is the most basic activity for anyone with two legs and is probably the best for people who are middle-aged and/or severely out of shape. Dr Harry Johnson of the Life Extension Institute recommends walking as the only form of exercise for his middle-aged patients. He advises three brisk twenty minute walks every day (or two thirty-minute walks or one one-hour walk). When his patients ask him where they can find the time for this, he asks them, "Where do you find the time to eat three meals a day?" If your muscles are badly deteriorated, of course, it may take you weeks or months to get yourself in shape to take a brisk two-to-three-mile walk, but it's well worth making the effort. As Dr Morehouse says:

"Muscles are the engines that move you. The fuels for the engines are chemicals the body constantly renews. These fuels are useless unless they have engines that are capable of functioning. If you don't use a muscle, it wastes away until it all but disappears. Each fibre shrinks to almost nothing. Yet the moment you start to use it again, it's like breathing on a bed of coals. It lights up, ignites. If you're one who has let himself go for twenty years, just try walking around the block. It's like a miracle. Where you thought there was nothing, strength reappears."

Once you're in shape, staying there can be done easily. Dr Morehouse lists five activities necessary for minimum maintenance (preventing any physical deterioration):

1. Turn and twist your body joints to their near-maximum range of motion.
2. Stand for a total of two hours per day.
3. Lift something unusually heavy for five seconds.
4. Get your heart rate up to 120 beats a minute for at least three minutes.
5. Burn up 300 calories a day in physical activity.

Losing weight via exercise.

If you're athletically inclined or a demon for physical exertion, it's entirely possible, of course, to lose as much weight as you choose through exercise alone. This is the way boxers and football players reduce. If you do one hour per day of running, swimming or rowing (briskly, at 1,000 calories per hour), you'll lose two pounds a week. Strenuous exercise, of course, should only be done by people who are young enough and healthy enough to stand it.

"Cost" of various activities in calories.

Walking slowly
120

Running
(depending on speed)
800-1,500

Dancing
300-450

Walking very fast
400-500

Tennis
400-500

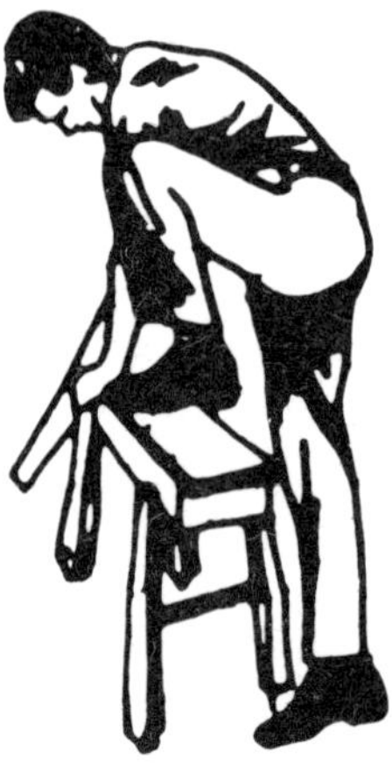

Sawing wood
300-400

Gardening
150-300

Carpentry
150-300

Housepainting
150-180

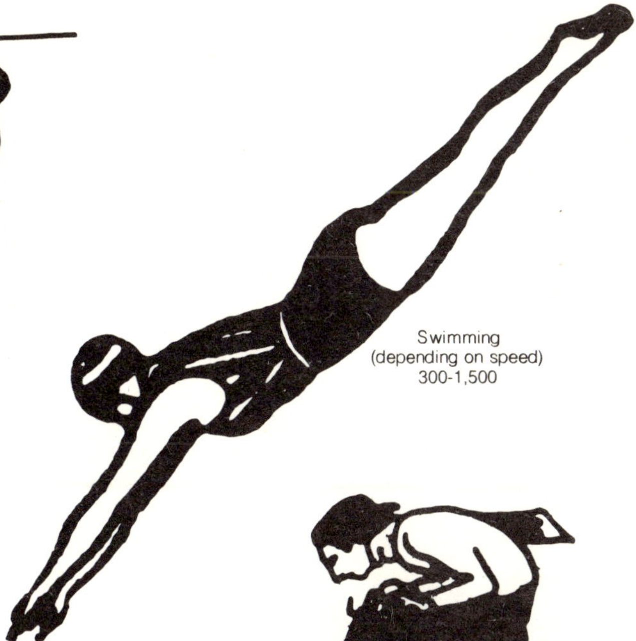

Swimming
(depending on speed)
300-1,500

Sweeping
80-100

Bicycling
(depending on speed)
250-450

Rowing
1,000-1,500

Reducing diets for drinkers.
The most famous is the "Drinking Man's Diet", essentially the same plan as those propounded by Dr Herman *(Calories Don't Count)* Taller, Dr Irwin *(The Doctor's Quick Weight Loss Diet)* Stillman, and Dr Robert *(Dr Atkins Diet Revolution)* Atkins. These all restrict the diet to protein, fat and roughage, plus 30 grammes or less of carbohydrates per day. Eat all the meat, fish, cheese, cottage cheese and butter you want and all the low-carbohydrate vegetables – leafy green vegetables, tomatoes, cauliflower, mushrooms, etc. – but nothing starchy or sweet. Drink all the distilled spirits you want and all the dry table wine, but no beer, which contains carbohydrates, or any wine or liquor with sugar in it. I've tried this diet and have talked to at least thirty other drinkers who have also, and found no one who lost as much as he wanted to, although some of the heavier people lost as much as twenty-five pounds. I lost about ten pounds (I wanted to lose thirty) and was unable to take off any more even though I persisted on the diet. By this time I was feeling quite uncomfortable and had acute cravings for fruit and potatoes, so I quit.

There are two problems with the low-carbohydrate, high-fat, high-protein diets. One is that because they are so unbalanced they tend to be unhealthy for some people – the high cholesterol content may be bad for people with a tendency to heart problems, for instance. The other difficulty is that the diet does not re-educate the appetite but encourages the dieter to gorge on less fattening substances.

There are many "crash" diets designed to take off a lot of weight in a short time, and they work. Having lost the weight, however, most crash dieters put it right back on again.

Many weight-control authorities are of the opinion that only a slow and gradual programme of weight reduction will result in permanent loss. Drastic diets are unsettling to the metabolism and do not allow the dieter to become thoroughly habituated to a lesser calorific intake. When the diet ceases, he will tend to revert to his previous eating habits. Dr Harry Johnson advises not changing one's eating habits or worrying about how many calories one consumes, but simply cutting out about 300 calories daily. In other words, count only the calories you eliminate. It doesn't much matter whether what you eliminate is fat, carbohydrate, alcohol, or even protein. This regime will produce a gradual loss – of about two to three pounds per month.

Cutting down on alcohol vs. cutting down on food.
Which is better? Probably it would be best for your health to eliminate mostly alcohol calories. But if you're at all concerned with permanent weight loss, you have to consider that if you start drinking again you'll regain what you lost. Cutting out food is not good either – you can't starve yourself indefinitely. Restricting both alcohol and food would seem to be the answer. How much of each depends on what you're currently consuming. Let's take two examples: A, a 160-pound man who is eating too much – 2,700 food calories plus 405 drink calories or 3,105 in all, and B, another 160-pound man who drinks too much – 1,500 food calories plus 1,445 alcohol calories, or 2,945 in all. Both need to cut down to 2,400 calories daily, but A should cut only a drink or two from his regime and take the rest of the calories from his food intake, and B should keep on eating at his present rate and cut down on alcohol calories only.

6. It can damage your health.

Drink can make you sick, change your life, or shorten it. Here are some of the major risks that the heavy drinker should face up to.

There is no question that the heavy and/or prolonged drinking of alcohol can be a threat to health and, ultimately, to life itself. So, in varying degrees, are smoking, lack of exercise, obesity and lack of proper nutrition. Psychologically negative conditions such as general unhappiness, depression, tension, anxiety, chronic rage and frustration (sexual or otherwise) can contribute to the hazard also. The more these other conditions are present together with alcohol, the greater the threat to health and life span.

It has been estimated that excessive drinking removes ten to twenty years from the normal life expectancy. Empirically, this estimate seems more or less correct, if one looks at all the drinkers who die in their sixth decade (or before) rather than in the seventh or eighth. For every Winston Churchill who lives into ripe old age despite a heavy alcohol habit, there would appear to be thousands of others whose drinking shortens their lives.

Thus, unless you sincerely consider that dying of drink is a glorious way to go (which it isn't, especially towards the end), it would be well to think of cutting down to a sensible intake sometime during the fourth decade of your life, or most certainly the fifth. Frequent checkups by a doctor, preferably one who's had a lot of experience with the health problems of drinkers, are also indicated. Let's look at some of the health hazards that drinkers may encounter.

Alcohol and your liver.

The liver is the largest gland in the body, a complex chemical factory which serves as a source of fuel for the organism, a waste-disposal system removing toxins and impurities from the blood, a manufacturer of hormones and enzymes, and has many other functions besides. The liver is a busy organ. It converts starch into glycogen, then stores it, releasing the glycogen for energy as it is needed. It breaks down protein into amino acids, stores fat and vitamins, destroys and recycles old blood cells, releases antibodies into the bloodstream . . . and handles the metabolism of alcohol.

The average adult liver weighs about four pounds and is located in the right upper abdomen, directly below the diaphragm. In a healthy state, it does not protrude beneath the ribs. Under the influence of too much alcohol, however, it can increase enormously in size, sometimes virtually filling the right side of the abdomen. One of the admirable characteristics of the liver is its reserve capacity. As much as two-thirds of its cells can be destroyed yet the remainder will carry out all the required functions. The liver also has amazing powers of regeneration. Given a rest of a few days or weeks from whatever poison has been destroying it – in our case alcohol – it will grow back to its former size and efficiency.

The primary effect of alcohol is to produce fatty liver. This is not a long-drawn-out process, but occurs instantly on ingestion of alcohol. The liver stops burning its normal fuel, which is fat, and switches to the alcohol instead. Ingesting just 1 oz of spirits (a single whisky) will raise the fat content of the liver from a normal 3% to about 3½%. Further drinks will increase the fat content accordingly. One need not be an alcoholic or heavy drinker to develop fatty liver – regular moderate drinkers have it also. Fatty liver is not a disease in itself, simply a condition which may or may not lead to health-threatening complications.

No causal relationship between fatty liver and actual liver diseases such as alcoholic hepatitis and cirrhosis has been demonstrated. Although heavy drinking almost invariably deposits excess fat in the liver, only a tiny minority of heavy drinkers develop cirrhosis. It is therefore thought that moderate or intermittent fatty liver probably does not in itself lead to cirrhosis. Since cirrhosis is definitely associated with prolonged heavy drinking, however, it is likely that the burden placed on the organ by extreme fattiness, plus perhaps other factors not presently known, does bring about the disease. The whole process is not yet well understood.

Alcoholic hepatitis is an inflammation of the liver brought about by excessive drinking, usually over a period of years, plus probably a deficiency of protein and vitamins in the diet. (An adequate protein intake tends to protect the liver from damage by alcohol.) The symptoms of hepatitis are fever (usually), an elevated white-blood-cell count, pain in the upper right abdomen and jaundice. The disease may or may not be associated with fatty liver or cirrhosis. It usually subsides when drinking is stopped, although occasionally a patient dies of liver failure or goes on to contract cirrhosis even though he has discontinued his use of alcohol.

One case I'm familiar with is of a hard-drinking friend who developed hepatitis over twelve years ago. He was hospitalized for several weeks and on his release his physician advised him to avoid alcohol entirely for at least two years. He stuck to teetotalism for only a couple of months, however, then went back to drinking. He is still in perfect health, despite this flouting of doctor's orders. Possibly what has kept him from any recurrence of liver trouble is the fact that he no longer drinks every day. Although still a heavy drinker, he confines his drinking to one or two days at the weekend. This intermittency of intake, allowing the liver to rest and regenerate between drinking bouts, may have been enough to keep him well. (I tell this story to illustrate the recuperative powers of the liver, not to urge hepatitis convalescents to follow the example of my rash friend. He was lucky; in his place many others might have suffered severe relapses.)

Cirrhosis. When damage to the liver, from whatever cause (these causes can include, besides alcohol, poor nutrition, infection, gallstone complications and heart failure), becomes so severe that scarring occurs, the result is cirrhosis. The liver ceases to function properly. The scarring produces a damming effect which impedes the flow of blood in the liver. Bypassing the liver, the circulatory system then begins to return blood directly from the intestinal tract to the general system, with the impurities that would normally be removed still present. The abdominal cavity begins to fill with fluid (dropsy). The patient's arms and legs become spindly and malnourished. In males, testicles atrophy and breasts enlarge. Females suffer a cessation of menstrual periods and their breasts may either enlarge or shrink away. All these symptoms can be reversed by stopping drinking, provided the scarring has not progressed to the point where the liver is no longer able to regenerate. Once cirrhosis has become fully established, however, the disease is fatal.

How much drinking does it take to produce cirrhosis? The most thorough study of the relationship between alcohol intake and cirrhosis is one done by Professor G. Pequignot, of France, in 1961. Professor Pequignot's figures are as follows:

1. Harmless use of alcohol	up to 80 grammes per day (3 oz 70° proof spirits)
2. Risk zone	80 to 160 grammes (3-6 oz)
3. Great risk	more than 160 grammes (6 oz)

According to both Pequignot and another researcher, Dr W. K. Lelbach, of the University of Bonn, persons who drink about 16 oz of whisky or more daily for twenty years stand about a 50-50 chance of developing cirrhosis. Below this level of intake, the chances of cirrhosis drop sharply, although the disease can and does also strike extremely moderate drinkers. As the risk table above clearly demonstrates, the danger area begins at a much lower level of intake (see also Dr Howard's comments at the end of the chapter).

Alcohol and your heart

Although alcohol does seem to provide at least some degree of protection against atherosclerosis and coronary heart disease, its role in another type of heart ailment, cardiomyopathy, is anything but helpful. Fortunately, this disease is usually confined to persons with a long history of ultra-heavy drinking. As opposed to coronary heart disease, cardiomyopathy is not due to circulatory problems but to a weakening of the heart muscle itself. The heart becomes enlarged, the neck veins distended; there is a narrow pulse pressure, elevated diastolic blood pressure, and œdematous swellings of the limbs. This condition is identical to nutritional cardiomyopathy (one of the symptoms of beri-beri, caused by deficiency of the B vitamins, particularly B1) but some researchers in recent years have attempted to show that myopathy (weakness and deterioration of the muscles) can be produced by alcohol alone. Though their arguments are not totally convincing to nutritionists (whose criteria for a "good" or "adequate" diet are rather stringent), the fact remains that cardiomyopathy is a very serious disease. Any drinker experiencing a sudden or gradual weakening of the muscles should consult a doctor or cardiologist forthwith.

The French have long congratulated themselves on their relative immunity to atherosclerosis and coronary heart disease, which they ascribe to *le bon vin*. But from Dr Kurt Oster, Chief of

Cardiology at Park City Hospital in Bridgeport, Connecticut, comes an intriguing new hypothesis which would ascribe the Frenchman's cardiac health not so much to his wine as to his milk. Dr Oster believes that atherosclerosis is caused not by cholesterol-containing animal fat, but by an enzyme called xanthine oxydase. This enters the system when we drink cow's milk, which contains xanthine oxydase (human milk does not). No xanthine oxydase can be absorbed from milk which has been curdled or preboiled (killing the enzyme) and only small quantities could be directly absorbed from ordinary whole milk (the enzyme particles being mostly too large to be absorbed through bood vessel walls); but when milk is homogenized, the smaller size of the particles enables the xanthine oxydase to enter the bloodstream and attack heart and arteries. This would seem to be an interesting theory only, were it not for the fact that heart disease does appear to increase in proportion to the consumption of whole and especially of homogenized milk.

Let's compare figures for the four nations with the most heart attacks and the four with the least.

Heart disease and milk consumption.

Country	Atherosclerosis Death Rate per 100,000	Milk Consumption (in pounds per person)	Homogenized	Preboiled
Finland	244.7	593	33%	No
United States	211.8	273	almost all	No
Australia	204.6	304	15%	No
Canada	187.4	288	part	No
Switzerland	75.9	370	small quantity	Yes
Sweden	74.7	374	—	Yes
France	41.7	230	—	Yes
Japan	39.1	48	some	—

Notice that Finland, by far the largest milk consumer, leads in deaths. The United States, where virtually no un-homogenized whole milk is sold, is second. All four high-death-rate countries use unboiled whole milk. Of the four countries with low death rates, three preboil their milk and the fourth, Japan, uses cow's milk much less than do the Western nations.

Alcohol and the brain

A number of experiments has shown that brain damage can be induced in laboratory animals by exposure to alcohol. Apparently alcohol interferes with the metabolism of the brain in ways which we don't yet fully understand. Similar experimentation on humans is of course impossible (thankfully) but alcoholic brain damage in humans can be confirmed.

Drs Ben Morgan-Jones and Oscar A. Parsons, of the University of Oklahoma Health Services Center, recently made some experiments which confirm that chronic drinkers behave like patients with verified brain damage. To test their subjects, they gave the Halstead Category Test, a geometrical concept-forming task which measures frontal-lobe damage, to 120 adults at a Veterans Hospital. Forty of the subjects were dried-out male alcoholics, 40 were patients with brain damage, and 40 were a control group with no alcoholic or neurological history. They reported their experiment in an article in *Psychology Today:*

"Since older people generally don't do so well on this test as younger people, we divided each group into old and young patients. The results confirmed our original suspicion. The young alcoholics performed nearly as well as the young controls, whereas young alcoholics and young controls got better scores than the young brain-damaged patients. The older alcoholics, as expected, performed somewhat like the older brain-damaged patients, while both these groups did much worse than the older controls.

"We discovered that the longer a person had been an alcoholic, the more his scores suffered. The results of a later study showed that excessive drinking for more than eight years would impair a person's abstracting and conceptualizing abilities. Still another test, in which we asked alcoholics to turn a knob as slowly as possible, satisfied us that they were unable to exert as much inhibitory control over their motor behaviour as were non-alcoholics."

This brain deterioration is by no means uniform for all drinkers, however. Dr Parsons told me that while his studies have led him to believe that anyone drinking a pint (16 oz) of liquor a day over a period of years would probably incur significant brain damage, he has nevertheless tested quart-a-day drinkers who came through his tests with flying colours. He has no opinion on why some drinkers seem to have escaped brain damage while others succumb.

Another, though less conclusive, finding of the Jones-Parsons studies is that although long-term alcoholics are just as intelligent verbally as non-alcoholics, some aspects of their non-verbal, spatial and visual performance seem to be decidedly inferior. "This suggests that the usually dominant left hemisphere of the brain, which is primarily responsible for language, suffers less than the right hemisphere, which appears to be more responsible for non-verbal information processing, including the recognition of shapes and tones and the analysis of spatial and tactile patterns," say Jones and Parsons. In other words, a highly verbal chronic drunk may appear to be of unimpaired intelligence while actually he's deteriorated in ways that don't show.

Do "normal" drinkers get brain damage too?

There is no firm answer to this question, but I don't think in general that tests made on alcoholics are necessarily "exportable" to the rest of the drinking population. The type of alcoholic used in medical experiments is someone who has demonstrated that he is unable to handle liquor. He has been hospitalized, perhaps repeatedly; has spent long periods of his life in Stages Three and Four; has perhaps suffered attacks of delirium tremens and other destructive conditions; has usually lived for long periods of time with totally inadequate nutrition.

A voice from the morgue.

I asked Dr Milton Helpern, former Chief Medical Examiner of New York City and a man who has probably conducted more autopsies than anyone else in his profession, whether he had observed signs of brain atrophy in alcoholic cadavers. He said that atrophy, not only of the frontal lobes but of the entire brain, was quite common in alcoholics. The condition is apparent by the large collection of fluid on the surface of the brain – "peel oedema" (sometimes called "external hydrocephalus") – which is found when the skull is opened up. "The condition is only evident in the autopsy room. You see it on the surface of the brain when you're taking the skull cap off. Once the brain has been removed and placed in formalin for examination by a pathologist, however, evidence of atrophy can no longer be observed. This is why many pathologists, who work only on organs removed for them by technicians, are unfamiliar with alcoholic brain atrophy."

Alcoholics also show lesions in the "mammillary bodies" of the brain – Wernicke's syndrome, a deterioration of the brain due to acute vitamin B1 shortage. "There's no question that the brain suffers definite damage from alcoholism," says Dr Helpern. "Not all alcoholics show it, of course, just as not all of them show cirrhosis or fatty liver. But many do. You see a lot of muscle atrophy, too." Dr Helpern believes that only heavy and prolonged drinking can produce severe changes in the body. When he finds such changes in a body represented as having been that of a moderate drinker, he tends to feel that the person was, in fact, an alcoholic who drank more heavily than was reported.

Avoiding the hazards.

First, we know that heavy drinking over a period of years can produce serious diseases in drinkers. What constitutes dangerously heavy drinking? Well, if animal experiments are any guide, drinking is highly dangerous when alcohol constitutes 50% (or more) of the total calories in the diet. That is the ratio of alcohol to food that was successful in producing cirrhosis in an experiment with baboons. Anything approaching a 50-50 distribution between food and alcohol calories should be avoided, therefore. Probably 40% is too high also. An intake of two-thirds food calories to one-third alcohol calories, or less, would seem safer. Remember, though, we are talking here about upper limits rather than recommended daily rations, and so any regular diet should be pitched lower still. (For calorie tables see previous chapter.)

Second, we know that prolonged, day-after-day, year-after-year drinking of even moderate amounts can put a strain on the liver and other organs. So it would seem prudent to have a "dry" day every once in a while. New York cardiologist Dr Elliott J. Howard advises patients who take three or more drinks daily to abstain completely for two days a week "to allow the organs (liver, brain, heart) and muscles to 'detoxify' from the alcohol-breakdown products. Some day, when we are able to pinpoint the exact nature of the toxic reaction, we can be more specific in our advice. Meanwhile, as a conservative precautionary health measure, periodic abstention seems a wise course."

7. It can make you an alcoholic.

What it means to be so dependent that you can't do without drink. The roles of guilt and fear. Alcohol and the addictive personality.

Many drinkers tend to worry about whether or not they are alcoholics, or incipient or borderline alcoholics, or in danger of becoming so. So let's go into this question.

Is an alcoholic someone who often staggers when he walks? Someone with a lot of empty whisky bottles in his dustbin? Someone who drinks more than a certain amount? Someone who likes to drink alone, or in the morning? Someone who's often late to work because he is hung over? Someone who acts weird or goes berserk after a couple of drinks? Someone who always gets blotto at parties?

Consider: George and Mary like to drink and in fact they drink a lot. Martinis begin flowing as soon as George gets home from work, wine or more drinks are served at dinner, and after dinner the couple continue to imbibe until falling-down drunk. Often they have guests, friends who drink just as heartily as they do. At work, George often brags about what a monumental hangover he has, and everyone chuckles sympathetically. George works in an occupation which looks favourably upon liquor. If once in a while he happens to get spifflicated at lunch, his boss and colleagues are quite understanding – after all, it could, and does, happen to them also. Mary gets her children off to school on time every morning, keeps her house clean and tidy, and in general is regarded as a model member of the community. In fact, she was chairman of the PTA last year and is a leading light in the local community. Are George and Mary alcoholics? Not to themselves, their friends, George's employers, or the community at large. True, there are people who would regard them as alcoholics, but those people are not part of George and Mary's crowd. Put another way, alcohol may kill them in the end, but George and Mary get by *socially*.

Sidney drinks less than George does, but his wife Lucy, and most of their friends, are teetotallers. Lucy had an uncle who was "taken by the booze", and has hated alcohol ever since. When Sidney exhibits signs of drunkenness at family gatherings, Lucy is deeply ashamed and everyone else looks the other way, trying to ignore the disgrace of it all. Sidney feels quite guilty after one of these episodes. Twice in the last ten years, Lucy has had him committed briefly as an alcoholic and once she had him arrested, when he slapped her during a marital argument.

Although Sidney's boss has no strong opinions, for or against, about drinking, he has heard about all this and watches his employee closely for signs of his going "out of control". Sidney does his job perhaps a little better than George does his, but he will never be promoted to a key position in his company. To his wife, his friends, his employer, even to himself, Sidney is an alcoholic.

"Alcoholism" is an example of what the eminent sociologist Erving Goffman calls "the insanity of place". We might call it inappropriate drunkenness. Someone who shows up drunk in church, or in court, is out of place, whereas someone drunk at a cocktail party is usually not. This leads us to a sociological definition of alcoholism: an "alcoholic" is someone who, by drinking, breaks social rules or fails to adhere to social rituals generally accepted in his milieu. By itself this is only a partial definition; but there are many other views to consider.

What about medical definitions?

No one can deny that there are many sick people who drink and many people who have made themselves sick by drinking. But is there any such thing as a progressive disease of drinking, brought about by drinking, called alcoholism? No, not in any definition that makes sense. I invite any reader who doubts this statement to read a book called *The Disease Concept of Alcoholism*, by E. M. Jellinek. Meticulously researched and presented with admirable fairness, the book reviews all the arguments ever made pro and con the disease concept of alcoholism and all the explanations or "etiologies" suggested for such a disease, none of which is entirely convincing or satisfactory to the author. The one argument that he does find convincing is as follows. After acknowledging that there is no clear-cut-definition of the term "disease", Dr Jellinek goes on:

"Pointing out this lack of definition of disease by no means involves a reproach. The splendid progress of medicine shows that this branch of the sciences can function extremely well without such a definition. Physicians know what belongs in their realm.

It comes to this, that a disease is what the medical profession recognizes as such. The fact that doctors are not able to explain the nature of such a condition does not constitute proof that it is not an illness. There are many instances in the history of medicine of diseases whose nature was unknown for many years. The nature of some is still unknown, but they are nevertheless unquestionable medical problems.

. . . the medical profession has officially accepted alcoholism as an illness, whether a part of the lay public likes it or not, and even if a minority of the medical profession is disinclined to accept the idea."

Elsewhere in his book, Dr Jellinek gives an all-purpose definition of alcoholism: any use of alcoholic beverages that causes any damage to the individual or society or both. He makes the statement deliberately vague in order to encompass all possible notions of alcoholism. In Anglo-Saxon areas, for instance, as we saw in Chapter 2, the generally accepted version of an alcoholic is someone who craves liquor and who, once he's taken one drink, cannot stop until he's totally blotto. Some students of Anglo-Saxon alcoholism, however, would include under the term heavy week-end drinkers as well as "relief drinkers" who never become "addicted". In France, the heaviest-drinking nation in the world, there is little overt drunkenness of the Stage Three or Stage Four variety. Instead, the average Frenchman consumes from two to three litres of wine throughout the day, maintaining a state in which he is never really drunk, yet is never quite sober. Without ever showing much drunkenness, French alcoholics do contract all the classic alcoholic ills – delirium tremens, cirrhosis, Wernicke's syndrome, and so on. The French alcoholic is said to be *alcoolisé* – alcoholized.

In the "hard-liquor" zone of Northern Europe, where the sale of liquor is often restricted, alcoholism takes the form of explosive bouts of drinking, after which the participants may become violent, or pass out. Aware of the negative, anti-social nature of their drinking, the Swedish government is now seeking to re-educate people to recognize the damage that it can cause. One measure of the government's success is that some groups of Swedes will now contemplate hiring a minibus to take them out for an evening's drinking. Not only that, many get beyond thinking about it and actually hire the minibus. It may not seem much, but imagine trying to persuade a similar crowd of British drinkers – a darts team, say, going to an away match – to leave *all* their cars at home. Derisive laughter would be the almost automatic response to what would be seen as a slight on their collective virility and capacity for alcohol.

Yet drunken driving is a major social ill in Britain, the proven cause of such a high percentage of road accidents, many including fatalities, that the "Coursh I can drive" attitude cannot be morally defensible. To kill someone while drunk at the wheel, or anywhere else, is by itself no proof of alcoholism, but the effects of drunken driving are such that the present inability to cope with the problem does indicate a general blind-spot, a misplaced tolerance, which is perhaps typical of British attitudes to alcoholism.

The facts of drinking.

The facts of drinking are relatively straightforward. Increased or prolonged drinking leads to increased tolerance for alcohol, allowing the drinker to drink more and function more effectively in the drunken state than he initially could. Increased tolerance also leads to loss of control over one's drinking, since in the successive stages of drunkenness the drinker is unable to maintain sober or "conscious" control. In addition, drinking in the absence of proper nutrition produces multiple ills which may become quite severe, even fatal, and may induce discomfort which only further drinking can relieve. Furthermore, prolonged or excessive drinking of alcohol may produce possibly irreversible tissue damage. While we don't know everything about alcohol, certainly more is known about its effects and side effects than is known about many other drugs and medications in common use.

Given the present state of knowledge, it ought to be possible to diagnose and treat the various ills attendant on drinking in a sensible, rational way. But we're not rational about alcohol. There is always that whiff of brimstone, *frisson* of terror, hint of degradation, twinge of revulsion or pious desire to save someone from himself that occurs when the notion "alcoholic" enters in. Society is itself irrational and has always responded better to myths than realities.

This tendency to prefer dramatized or fictional versions of

reality to what actually happens was what in the past created the climate for the excesses of the abolitionists, who went around shrieking about the "crime-producing, food-wasting, youth-corrupting, home-wrecking" effects of liquor. Nowadays, when asked to think about addiction of one kind or another, we still prefer to take our evidence from made-up sources, for example Ray Milland's bender in *The Lost Weekend,* or Frank Sinatra's *Man With the Golden Arm,* instead of maybe watching a documentary that introduces real-life characters and their problems. We recoil from the latter, protesting that it's "too near the knuckle" or, more revealing, that it's "not entertainment", as though we can only be serious about things that don't actually happen.

In Britain, as attitudes to drinking and driving indicate, people are on the whole slow to condemn anti-social behaviour. The historic regard for personal freedoms shown in Britain is admirable, and is regularly envied by people in other nations. Another national trait is less admirable, however. This is the tendency to be complacent, to put faith in the *status quo* often for no better reason than that, by definition, it is there. Certainly, in the way the British look at – or fail to look at – the pitfalls of excessive social drinking, there is room for greater alertness and greater willingness to act.

Unfortunately, as we have said, there is an inbred abhorrence of "addiction" and "alcoholism" that is counter-productive. Instead of actively looking for help, the "problem drinker" hides away in his or her shame. In Britain today many bodies give useful advice on drink and alcoholism. One of these, the London Council on Alcoholism, defines "problem drinking" in very simple terms. It is the kind of drinking that is:

"taking up more time than is socially appropriate,
being used to lift one's spirits constantly,
cutting into the budget,
causing family/friends to become concerned,
interfering with road safety,
interfering with any aspect of work,
interfering with health."

This of course does not define an out-and-out alcoholic – it isn't meant to – but it does describe an emerging alcoholic, and the stage at which he or she should seek help.

The role of guilt and fear.

Since this book is aimed at the normal social drinker rather than the alcoholic or "problem drinker", I made no attempt to seek out people who felt they had drinking problems. I did encounter some, however, and in talking to them I was struck by a certain pattern of self-doubt and self-castigation that cropped up in all their conversations. "Drinking's a filthy habit," one man told me. "I don't know why I do it. I become disgusting when I drink, just like a beast. [Something I've failed to observe, though I've seen him drunk.] I was much better off when I was on the wagon."

I talked with a girl in her early twenties who feels she has a drinking problem because she has had blackouts after drinking and while drunk has made phone calls and written letters that were bolder and/or more hostile than she liked to think about when sober. This girl's parents had both been alcoholics, and she had a deep fear of ending up "like them".

Another man told me, "I have self-destructive tendencies, I know that. That's what my drinking is all about. I just hope I don't end up in Bellevue or on the Bowery someday." This was a prosperous advertising executive whose drinking seems to an outsider unexceptional and well controlled.

Self-doubt, ambivalence and guilt feelings about drinking, and a fear of alcoholism seem to be universal among people who feel they have a drinking problem. There are members of Alcoholics Anonymous who joined in their teens or early twenties after a very limited drinking experience and have remained members ever since. What drinking they did threw a scare into them from which they have not recovered. Some people don't even need to drink at all to arrive at a similar conclusion. I've heard several non-drinkers say that the reason they don't touch alcohol is that "I just know I'd turn into an alcoholic if I did."

Three of the normal drinkers I interviewed – two men and one woman, all in their forties – told me that at one point in their lives they had become worried that their drinking was turning into alcoholism and had joined AA. Later they decided their worries were baseless and went back to drinking again.

Helping the alcoholic.

If we accept the notion that an alcoholic is someone who acknowledges (or imagines) that he is drinking in a self-destructive way, we still are faced with the problem of what to do for him. The traditional approach – treating alcoholism as a unitary process or disease caused by drinking – has the defect that it blames drinking for the alcoholic's plight, and by so doing lumps together two factors that don't necessarily belong together. The physical and mental effects of excessive drinking are well known and can be cured and/or prevented (provided they are caught soon enough) by vitamin-mineral therapy plus adequate nutrition. But the other factor in alcoholism – the desire to drink self-destructively (or to fancy that one does) – is not inevitably connected to alcohol. Alcohol addicts could just as easily choose narcotics or barbiturates (many have at one time or another) to be the focus of their addiction – or gambling, or over-eating. The alcoholic is an addictive personality, someone with an urge to be dependent, and alcohol just happens to be the substance he has chosen for his dependency. Alcohol itself does not cause dependency. Let me quote from the book *Love and Addiction,* by Stanton Peele and Archie Brodsky:

"Addiction is not a chemical reaction. Addiction is an experience, one which grows out of an individual's routinized subjective response to something that has special meaning for him – something, anything, that he finds so safe and reassuring that he cannot be without it. So if we want to come to terms with addiction, we have to stop pointing the finger at drugs and start looking at people, at ourselves, and at what makes us dependent. We will find that we learn habits of dependence in part by growing up in a culture which teaches a sense of personal inadequacy, a reliance on external bulwarks, and a preoccupation with the negative or painful rather than the positive or joyous.

Our customary image of the dirty, despised "drug addict" or alcoholic is part of a general conception of addiction as an abnormality of our society. But in reality addiction is not an aberration from the norm; it is itself the norm. Drug dependency is a mirror-image of more basic dependencies that we learn at home and in school. The addict's search for a hollow, external resolution of life (whether through a drug or an escapist love affair) follows directly from the hollow, external relationships we are led to have with each other, with our minds and bodies, with the physical world, with learning and work and play. Those young people who suddenly repudiate convention and seek some ultimate solace in acid or speed, or a religious commune, are only expressing tendencies that were always present in the accepted guise of a superficial home and school life."

Medical science has the answer – a relatively simple one – to the effects of excessive drinking. Let it not also pretend it knows how to cure the desire to be dependent. That is something that only a spontaneous change of heart by the addict himself can accomplish. And only when we know more than we do at present about the nature of dependence, can we hope for more changes of heart.

Part three. The well-adjusted drinker.

8. Living with alcohol.

Make sure your drinking is under control. If you're overdoing it, and getting over-dependent, learn to get by on less.

If you have been drinking heavily for a while, it's surprising how much better you can feel after a day without drink plus a good night's sleep. The difference is tremendous – which is just as well, because it will encourage you to control your future intake.

It is probably fair to say that if you regard yourself as a moderate social drinker, you are drinking too much. And if you have been drinking for fifteen years or more, you almost certainly are overdoing it. Dependence on drink is something that can take many years to build up – then suddenly it becomes painfully obvious that you are more or less hooked. A lot of people in early middle age find themselves in this situation – and are surprised and shocked. Perhaps they have been upping their intake so gradually that they haven't really noticed; or maybe they are earning more money now and spending more on wine and spirits than they used to. Whatever the pattern, they are now more dependent than they find comfortable. It's time to do something, and the thing to do is to cut down on their drinking. Here are some suggested ways of going about it.

1. Be Honest About How Much You Drink. Make a real effort to establish *exactly* how much you are drinking. Chart yourself over a week, then over another week and take the average. Note down every drink you have, *and* how big it is. Remember, if you drink spirits at home it's unlikely that you are giving yourself the equivalent of pub singles; more probably you will be downing doubles, or even trebles, so it's an obvious cheat to put one of those down on your list as "1 whisky", without qualification. When you have arrived at an honest weekly total, resolve to cut it down by 20%. Devise ways to achieve your target. (This exercise ties in with Behaviour Modification, discussed later in this chapter.)

2. **Lunchtime.** If you are in the habit of drinking two or three drinks at lunch, have only one. Better still, cut out lunchtime drinking altogether. This can have the advantage of restricting your drinking to one period per 24 hours.
3. **The First Drink of the Evening.** Keep this as late as possible. The pubs usually open at 5.30 pm, and by 6 o'clock a lot of people, at home as well as in offices, have started muttering about yardarms, etc. So be superior – hold out till 7 o'clock, or later.
4. **No Pre-dinner Drinks.** A drastic limitation, maybe, but a very useful one. Don't drink during the day, or before dinner. Then limit your intake at dinner to two glasses of wine, or cider, or whatever you usually have. Then you can feel freer about drinking after dinner.
5. **Dry Days.** Pick out a day when it's convenient not to drink, and then announce, to yourself and others, "I never drink on Mondays [or whenever]." If you find this reasonably painless, add a second dry day.
6. **Go Without With Someone Else.** This is easier to administer in the home. Couples simply agree to postpone the first drink until the same hour, and have their dry days together. You can follow this course with a friend or office colleague, though it's probably best if you are actually together while performing your rite of abstention.
7. **Become a Connoisseur.** Stop buying the cheapest brands of wine or whisky by the caseful, and invest in a bottle or two of something good. Sip your drinks and savour the difference.

Dealing with craving.

The theory has been put forward that there is no such thing as a craving for something. There is only craving, in general. According to this theory, if there is such a thing as a specific craving shared by all mankind, it is the craving for permanency of desire. Craving, in other words, is not wanting something, it is wanting to want something. In the midst of eternal chaos, our idiot minds desire permanence, security, order. One way to get these is to find something that magically always satisfies, always fulfills. This might be a steak, a cigarette, a drink, a mystical religious experience, sex, anything. Logan Pearsall Smith wrote that his idea of heaven on earth would be to read and forget, re-read and re-forget, endlessly, the novels of Jane Austen.

Craving has a way of making the craver more real to himself.

He's not just a human cipher, a jellyfish – he wants something, by God! Craving can only be done in the absence of the craved object, or when that object is prohibited. Sitting in his kitchen with a refrigerator full of bottles, a beer drinker does not crave beer. It's only when, for instance, he's out in the hot sun miles from anywhere that he starts to miss it. Similarly, the cigarette smoker only craves a smoke when he wakes up in the middle of the night and finds he's out of cigarettes, or after he's decided to quit the smoking habit.

Another characteristic of craving is that it's an obsession, something the craver broods about constantly. Any unusual condition of body or mind – a twinge of self-doubt, a feeling of bodily discomfort, a change of mood, etc. – is interpreted as a desire for the craved object. The smoker thinks he wants a smoke, the drinker a drink, the sex fiend sex.

Craving is a form of self-brainwashing. Just as the lover will "psych" himself up for an assignation with his mistress by dwelling mentally on her charms for hours beforehand, a drinker will spend a lot of time thinking about how good the first drink of the day is going to taste. Often this is a communal activity, with several drinkers egging each other on to lust after booze: "I bet I know what George is thinking about. A large G and T. Eh, George?"

In dealing with craving it's good to remember that it's unreal, a trumped-up condition you've programmed yourself into. The way to handle craving is not to resist it or give in to it, but to experiment with it. Say you're used to having a drink first thing when you get home from the office. You crave that drink, feel physically in need of it, look forward to it as a big event of the day. You know that that craving consists of (a) a stimulus, some sort of feeling of lack, and (b) an answer to that stimulus, such as "I need a drink."

Instead of responding to the obvious and taking a drink, try something new. Perhaps part of your "need" for a drink is simply that you're thirsty, so take a drink of water. Maybe you're feeling a little frazzled because your blood sugar is low: in that case eat something sweet. Possibly you're hungry and really crave the hors d'oeuvres that come with the drinks, so eat and don't drink. Perhaps you're tense and need to unwind: do something that will relax you – go for a brisk walk, mow the lawn, call up an amusing friend and have a long conversation, make love to your wife, read a good book, take a nap . . . In short, feed your craving something other than alcohol. You may find that it's just as well satisfied, for the moment, at least.

When you do drink, pay attention to your reactions. Are you enjoying the drink, does it taste good, did you really want it, do you feel better after having had it, or worse? Are you experiencing the actual drink, or an image of some imaginary, idealized ambrosia? Many drinkers have spent so much time pretending to like booze that they no longer have the slightest idea whether they really enjoy drinking or not. The pretence of enjoyment is part of the drinking ritual.

How to get less drunk.

In Chapter 2 we talked about the difficulties of trying to stay moderately immoderate. It's relatively easy to decide to have only one or two drinks and adhere to the decision, but how can you keep a resolve such as "I'm only going to get slightly drunk, not really drunk!" By the time you're mildly smashed the party spirit has reached you and you're impatient with that tiresome fellow – the sober, boring you – who's so hung up on moderation. Ignoring him, you pour yourself a few more stiff ones and become thoroughly bombed.

Is it possible for Sober You to give Drunk You instructions and have him carry them out? Yes, to a certain extent, if you remember that Drunk You is a different person who doesn't have all your awareness when sober, and doesn't respond, necessarily, to the same arguments you respond to. It's like sending a small child on an errand – you don't give him all sorts of complicated instructions he's liable to forget; you tell him very simply and clearly what to do. Let's say you're going to a party where you know hilarity will reign and the drink will flow very freely. You want to have some fun but would like to get home in a reasonably sober condition. This means you can drink yourself into Stage Two but certainly not beyond. You know what you want, but how do you persuade the Stage Two "you" to go along with your wish?

He's not as sensible as you are, remember. You can't just say to him, "Listen, we've been hitting the bottle rather too much lately, and in the interests of moderation I suggest we take it easy tonight. Besides, we have a nine-o'clock appointment tomorrow and we don't want to show up all hungover, do we? Therefore I think you ought to take it easy. If you notice you're getting at all out of hand during the evening, just switch to plain soda for a while, okay?" That's no way to talk to Stage Two. He's an expansive fellow who likes to think of himself as slightly larger than life. You can ask him to perform a heroic mission, but not some niggling little act of self-denial or self-assessment. Talk to him like this, "Look, I want you to do something very important for me. Very important! Listen carefully, here's what I want you to do: When you get to the party, you're to drink exactly two drinks per hour,* no more. Got that? One drink every half hour. One at nine, one at nine-thirty, one at ten . . . is that clear? Got your watch on? Is it all wound up? Look at it every time, okay? You know why this is so important? Because they say we're a couple of piss-artists, you and I. They say we can't possibly drink and not get crocked. Well, we're going to show them, right? Two drinks per hour. Don't let me down, now. I know I'm going to be proud of you when the party's over."

The drunken self is impatient of petty details but will attend to considerations that it deems urgent or important.

Some clues from "behaviour modification".

In the last few decades, the behavioural psychologist B.F. Skinner and his followers have evolved a system of modifying human and animal behaviour that can be used for everything from teaching pigeons to pilot missiles to re-educating autistic children to rehabilitating alcoholics – and it works. (The main criticism of behaviour modification is, in fact, that it works too well, and should not be used on people without their consent.) So let's see if it can give us some ideas for controlling how much we drink.

"Behaviour mod" is almost absurdly simple. It is concerned only with behaviour, not thoughts, feelings or motivations. A behaviour modification practitioner wouldn't care why you drink, for instance; he'd only be interested in how much and how often. He'd probably have you count exactly how many drinks you take each day and record the number on weekly or monthly charts. If craving for drink or obsession with drink is one of your problems, he'd have you carry around a little pocket counter and click it once every time the thought of liquor crosses your mind; how many times a day: five, ten, fifty, a hundred? These numbers too would be recorded on a chart. You would now have a quantitative picture of the behaviour you want to change. Also, the mere fact

*Or whatever other amount you calculate will keep him safely in Stage Two.

of knowing the extent of the problem might produce a certain feedback and influence you to lessen your frequency of drinking or thinking about drinking.

Behaviour, the "mod" people say, is controlled by reinforcement. If a certain piece of behaviour has good or pleasant, rewarding consequences, people tend to repeat it. If it has unpleasant or boring consequences, they do not. Good consequences are called positive reinforcement, bad ones negative reinforcement. One might call this reward and punishment, but that would distort the process somewhat. Reinforcement is unitary, with positive reinforcement leading to greater frequency of the reinforced behaviour and negative reinforcement leading to lesser frequency and finally extinction. As an example of the latter, if you had to walk three miles every time you wanted a shot of alcohol, you'd soon quit drinking.

Negative reinforcement cannot produce a desired pattern of behaviour; it can only extinguish an undesired one. It can reduce the frequency of undesired behaviour, but will not produce greater frequency of an alternative desired pattern.

The trouble with all this is that the world is constantly reinforcing undesirable behaviour and not reinforcing the desirable. For instance, when you stay sober nobody comes up and claps you on the back and tells you what a fine fellow you are. No, they take you for granted, perhaps even act as if you're somewhat boring. But when you get smashed and make an ass of yourself, all sorts of attention is paid to you – not all favourable, to be sure, but any form of attention is a tribute. You may squirm as they tell you all the terrible things you did last night, but at least they're talking about you.

How do you set behaviour modification to work on yourself? First, quantify your drinking. Keep a notebook and write down every drink you consume. You may not have a drink unless you mark it down. Second, make drinking more difficult. Don't keep liquor at your elbow: put it in the remotest room of your house, so that you have to make a trek to go and get a drink. Don't have the ice bucket and mixers handy to the booze, either. Put them somewhere else, so that you have to make two treks for each drink. Time your drinking, allowing yourself only one drink every half hour. Later lengthen that to one hour. At parties, don't walk around with your glass in your hand. Put it in some remote corner so you have to walk over to it every time you want a sip. And so on.

While you're doing all this, you also reward yourself for a diminishing frequency of drinking, and punish yourself for an increase. Figure out appropriate rewards and punishments. For instance, when you've been good you treat yourself to a new tie or eat out at your favourite restaurant. When you were bad you deprive yourself of watching a film you wanted to see, or are forced to send £5 to your least favourite charity.

Another behaviour modification technique is the contract. Actually this is a ploy that existed long before B.F. Skinner. In its simplest form, you bet somebody you can stay sober, or quit drinking entirely, for *x* amount of time. This works even better with two people who both want to cut down or quit. The ultimate contract is when you bet another drinker £50, or £100 – some amount that will really hurt – that you can stay on the wagon longer than he can.

Reinforcing the sober you.

If you're trying to cut your alcohol intake, it's probably because the joys of drunkenness or semi-drunkenness are wearing a little thin for you. Drinking less is a worthy goal, but also a rather negative one. So don't dwell too much on the thought of controlling your drinking. Concentrate instead on rediscovering the joys of sobriety. Note how pleasant it is to wake up with a clear head. Learn to enjoy having a sober mind with its alertness, its subtle interplay of thoughts and feelings too evanescent for the booze-deadened brain to apprehend. Get up early to observe a sunrise, or go bird watching. Take up something that demands sobriety, such as Transcendental Meditation, solving chess problems or building ship models out of toothpicks. Spend more time with children, animals and other creatures that know how to have fun without drinking. You've explored that dark world at the bottom of the bottle long enough (and it hasn't all been unworthwhile), but now come out into the clear light of day.

Appendix. If you need help.

If your drinking has got such a hold that you don't feel you can cope with the problem by yourself, there are plenty of things that you can do. First of all, seek professional advice. People often don't recognize that an alcoholic (which you may be) needs help that goes far beyond abstinence. Your local GP or social worker can advise you, or put you in touch with others who can help.

If you feel that they are too close to home territory, you can always contact one of the following organizations:

Alcoholics Anonymous.

This is a worldwide self-help group with some 800,000 members in 92 countries. It was co-founded by Bill Wilson and Robert Smith, both alcoholics, the latter an Ohio doctor. Wilson found that talking about his problem with other alcoholics gave him the strength to give up drinking. Anonymity is always preserved: this was a rule imposed by the founders, who were known as Bill W. and Dr Bob. Their main office in the UK is at: 11 Redcliffe Gardens, London, SW10 9BG. Tel: (01) 352 9779, or see your local telephone directory.

The National Council on Alcoholism.

The National Council operates a free service offering confidential information and advice on any drinking problem to anyone who consults them, either sufferers from alcoholism, problem drinkers, or anyone generally worried about their drinking. They also advise anyone who wishes to help an alcoholic or problem drinker, people such as husbands, wives, close relatives and friends. Their head office is at: 45 Great Peter Street, London, SW1P 3LT. Tel: (01) 222 1056/7.

There are affiliated regional councils, with information and advisory centres, in the following towns and cities:

Birmingham: Council on Alcoholism, 32 Essex Street, Birmingham B5 4TR. Tel: (021) 622 2041.

Bristol: Avon Council on Alcoholism, 14 Park Row, Bristol BS1 5LJ. Tel: (0272) 293028/9.

Canterbury: Kent Council on Alcoholism, 10 Station Road West, Canterbury CT2 8AN. Tel: (0227) 54740.

Coventry: & Warwickshire Council on Alcoholism, 5a Priory Row, Coventry CV1 5EX. Tel: (0203) 26619 & 26610.

Exeter: Devon Council on Alcoholism, 4 Wynards, Magdalen Street,

Exeter EX2 4HX. Tel: (0392) 55151.

Grimsby: Humberside Council on Alcoholism, St Andrew's Information and Advisory Centre, Albion Street, Grimsby DN32 7DY. Tel: (0472) 53416.

Leeds: Council on Alcoholism, 21/22 West Bar Chambers, 38 Boar Lane, Leeds LS1 5DB. Tel: (0532) 31029.

Liverpool: Merseyside Lancashire & Cheshire Council on Alcoholism, B15 The Temple, Dale Street, Liverpool L2 5RU. Tel: (051) 236 0300 & 1372.

London: Council on Alcoholism, 68 Chalton Street (side entrance), London NW1 1JR. Tel: (01) 387 2191 & 2214.

Manchester: Greater Manchester Council on Alcoholism, 4th Floor, 20 Princess Street, Manchester 1. Tel: (061) 236 3111.

Newcastle upon Tyne: North East Council on Alcoholism, Mea House, Ellison Place, Newcastle upon Tyne NE1 8XS. Tel: (0632) 20797.

Nottingham: Nottinghamshire Council on Alcoholism, 126 Mansfield Road, Nottingham. Tel: (0602) 56211, ext. 227.

Oxford: & District Council on Alcoholism, 75 Windmill Road, Headington, Oxford. Tel: (0865) 63295. Referrals Tel: (0865) 778050.

Southampton: Hampshire Council on Alcoholism, 18 West Park Road, Southampton SO1 0GA. Tel: (0703) 30219.

Swindon: Thamesdown & North Wilts. Council on Alcoholism, Dorothy House, 7 Temple Street, Swindon. Tel: (0793) 695405.

Taunton: Somerset Council on Alcoholism, Whirligig Lane, 12 Middle Street, Taunton. Tel: (0823) 88174.

Wellingborough – County of Northampton Council on Alcoholism, Bungalow 1, The Health Clinic, 18a Oxford Street, Wellingborough, Northants NN8 4JH. Tel: (0933) 223796.

South Wales Council on Alcoholism, Cardiff: Dyfrig House, Fitzhamon Embankment, Riverside, Cardiff CF1 8RN. Tel: (0222) 32127.

Newport: Emlyn House, 3 Palmyra Place, Newport, Gwent NPT 4EJ. Tel: (0633) 63185.

Channel Islands, Jersey: Council on Alcoholism, 19a James Street, St Helier. Tel: (0534) 26672.

Accept

A fairly new organization, whose initials represent the Alcoholism Community Care Centre for Education. Formed in 1975, it aims through a network of branches to offer therapeutic, practical and aftercare help "for people recovered from the illness of alcoholism". In January 1978 ACCEPT launched its "Early Recognition Campaign for Women". The Central office is at: Western Hospital, Seagrave Road, London, SW6. Tel: (01) 381 3155.